SERVING UNCLE SAM

IN THE 50TH OHIO

BY ERASTUS WINTERS

CORPORAL COMPANY K

1905

COPYRIGHT 2017 BIG BYTE BOOKS

DISCOVER MORE LOST HISTORY AT BIGBYTEBOOKS.COM

Contents

ERASTUS WINTERS 1
PUTTING ON THE BLUE 2
DRINKING FROM THE SAME CANTEEN 8
BATTLE OF PERRYVILLE 15
AFTER JOHN MORGAN 22
CAMP LIFE 30
A SMALL REBEL RAID 37
NEWS OF MORGAN'S CAPTURE 44
GLASGOW TO NASHVILLE TO GLASGOW 53
OVER THE CUMBERLAND MOUNTAINS 60
ON TO KNOXVILLE 70
WRITER STRIKES A SOFT SNAP 80
THE ATLANTA CAMPAIGN 89
STEALING A MARCH ON THE ENEMY 101
DEATH OF COLONEL ELSNER 110
HOOD TRIES TO CUT OUR HAVERSACK STRINGS 119
A NIGHT'S MARCH TO FRANKLIN 126
BATTLE OF FRANKLIN 135
HOW WE FARED UNDER THE STARS AND BARS 145
A TOUGH MARCH 150
CRUEL TREATMENT 156
A BREAK IN THE DARK CLOUDS AT LAST 166
FAREWELL TO CAHABA 175
DEATH OF PRESIDENT LINCOLN 186
INCIDENTS IN THE HOSPITAL 196
ARRIVE AT HOME 205

ERASTUS WINTERS

The Winters family of Ohio, like many families of the time, paid a terrible cost for their fidelity to the Union cause during the American Civil War. One son, Asa, was killed at the Battle of Richmond, Kentucky in 1862. Another son, Francis, had comparatively easy duty and was in service for only several months.

Then there was Erastus, our author. He was born on August 8, 1843, in Hamilton County, Ohio, ten miles northwest of Cincinnati, to Amos Winters and Mary Ann Pine. He not only survived disease (which killed many more men in the war than bullets), battle, and the Confederate prison camp at Cahaba, on the way home he survived what is still the worst maritime disaster in U.S. history—the sinking of the steamboat *Sultana*.

After the war, Winters worked in a number of occupations. He mentions in this book having been married and widowed three times. The first appears to have been to Rachel Hite in 1873. The second may have been either Mary E. Zard in 1882 or Ducena Chance in 1885. The third was Jennie Rigler in 1895. There was, however, a fourth marriage after this book was written. That was to Sarah Adaline Pierce in 1907.

In the 1900 federal census, just prior to writing this volume, he listed his occupation as "book agent." In 1910 he was living in a boarding house and listed under occupation, "own income." By 1920 he was retired.

Erastus Winters died in Ohio on March 25, 1925.

PUTTING ON THE BLUE

During the spring and summer of 1862, I was in the employ of a gentleman at College Hill, Ohio, near Cincinnati.

He was interested in the fruit business, and was putting out his entire farm in fruit. He took great pride in his trees, and labored among them daily, keeping their tops trimmed neat and uniform. He watched over and nursed them as tenderly as he did his children. Indeed, I admired his trees very much myself, as I worked, and put in a crop of navy beans among them, which were growing finely, when I left to enter the army. I shall have occasion to mention those trees again before I close this little story.

I kept myself posted in the progress of the war, and came to the conclusion that they would never be able to put down the rebellion without my assistance, and I spoke to my employer about it. Said he, "My boy, stay with me at moderate wages until I get my first crop of fruit, and I will make you a present of a fine young horse, saddle and bridle." I thanked him for his tempting offer, but said to him that I thought my services were needed in the army more than he needed them, and though I regretted to leave him and his good family, I bade them good bye.

When I told my parents my intentions, father bade me God speed, but mother objected very strongly, but I said to her if I remained at home, I was likely to be drafted, and asked her if she would not rather I would be a volunteer than to be forced into the service, besides that I would be with my cousin, who was a Lieutenant in the Company that I wished to join, and also that I would be with some of my chums, who had already enlisted, and with a lot more such talk as this, I finally overcame her objections, and she reluctantly gave her consent.

My parents at that time were living at Ludlow, Kentucky. I went over into Cincinnati, hunted up the recruiting office, and signed the roll as a member of Company "K," 50 Ohio Volunteers, and was sent out to Camp Dennison, and mustered into the United States Service for the period of three years, or during the war, receiving fifty dollars bounty [$1,350 in 2015] from Hamilton County, and twenty-five dollars cash from the Government, with a promise of seventy-five more at the close of my service.

The regiment at its organization was under the command of Colonel Jonah R. Taylor, Lieutenant Colonel Silas A. Strickland, Major Defrees and Adjutant George R. Elsner [sic; Elstner].

Company "K" was commanded by Captain L. A. Hendricks; First Lieutenant Oliver McClure; Second Lieutenant E. L. Pine; First Sergeant Charles Vanduezen [sic; Van Deursen], all fine looking officers. Vanduezen had been in the regular service, and was a number one drill master; as a result. Company "K" became in a short time very proficient in the manual of arms, and all company movements.

A few days after being mustered in, I was given a pass to visit my parents, brothers and sisters to bid them good bye, and receive their parting blessing. Yes, and I had a girl to leave behind me, and, of course, must see her, and bid her good bye also, and with a promise to write to her often, I bid her a sorrowful farewell. We corresponded regular for a few months, and then a young Methodist minister lay siege to her heart, and she became his for better or worse, but she was not the only pebble on the beach, and I did not remain long without another correspondent.

But to resume, returning to camp. After my pass expired, I was soon rigged out in a suit of Uncle Sam's blue, and armed with a musket, I began to think I was "It."

I was mustered into service, August 22, 1862, and after drilling squad company and regimental drill and standing guard until somewhere the first of September, we were ordered to Kentucky, and sent out the Lexington Pike near Fort Mitchell, and camped near the Highland House on an open lot for the night. Those that are well read in history will remember that this was the time that General Kirby Smith had invaded Kentucky, and was threatening Covington and Cincinnati. Nothing disturbed the quiet of our camp that night.

In the morning, several comrades with myself were detailed for fatigue duty, and were busy at work with pick and shovel just under the hill below camp; all went well for a short time, and then from headquarters came the nerve disturbing rattle of the long roll; beat with all the energy that Bob Crandle, our lame drummer boy could put in the drumsticks. We all understood what that meant—picks and shovels were dropped at once. I am not sure but those that had their picks in the air, ready to strike, left them hanging there, and we rushed to camp to find the regiment already forming on the parade ground. In the excitement, some comrade had mistaken my gun and accouterments for his own, but there is no time now for changing guns. I gather up what is left, and take my place at the head of Company "K," and at the command: Right, face, forward, double quick, march, we are off out the pike a short distance, file right through a. farm gate, then across fields, orchards, gardens, vineyards and vacant lots, jumping newly made breastworks.

We finally came to a halt with scarcely a half an inch of breath left inside the grim walls of old Fort Mitchell, where at that time, stood a battery of brass guns, the same that Professor Lloyd mentions in his famous book, *Stringtown on the Pike.*

John Uri Lloyd's 1901 novel of Kentucky. Fort Mitchell in Kentucky was one of seven fortifications built for the defense of Cincinnati during the Civil War.—Ed. 2017

I begin to look around now, and wonder where I am. As I glance along the line to right and left, I notice the boys' faces are very pale, caused no doubt by our great haste to reach the fort, or it may have been caused by the awful rattle of Bob's drum. Old veterans will all bear me out, I think in saying, the long roll is very trying on the nervous system, especially if it takes place in the vicinity of the enemy. So these two causes combined, I think, fully explains why our faces were so white at this particular time.

I don't wish to convey to the reader the impression that we were frightened; no, not by any means; we were just a bit nervous, that's all, but be that as it may, had we been called at that moment to give a specimen of our marksmanship, I fear that none of us would have hit the bull's eye. Our condition was something like the hunter who has run up on his first deer. We had what might be termed the "Buck Ague."

Half a mile or a mile south of Fort Mitchell, at that time the pike ran through a dense beech woods. We naturally looked out that direction after getting in the line in the fort, and we saw a great cloud of white dust arising above the tree tops; that settled it in our minds, of course, that the Rebel army under Kirby Smith was going to attack us, and it was their advance that was raising all that dust, so we kept our eyes fixed on that dust cloud, which drew nearer and nearer. Finally when we were all about ready to have nervous prostration, there emerges from that dark woods, not Kirby Smith's advance, but a large drove of government mules that were being driven in to save them from falling into the hands of Kirby Smith, whose advance was at Florence, only a few miles distant from Fort Mitchell, and his advance pickets and ours had exchanged a few shots at each other that morning, and a few men were killed and wounded as we learned afterwards.

Edmund Kirby Smith (1824–1893) was a career United States Army officer who became a Confederate general.—Ed. 2017

After these things calmed down, we returned to our camp near the Highland House, and this ended the bloodless battle of Fort Mitchell, and our first long roll experience.

There were thousands of men in the defenses of Covington at that time; raw recruits, militia and backwoods squirrel hunters; what kind of a fight we would have put up is hard to tell had Kirby Smith advanced on us, but he must have thought we were too many for him, for he flanked off to the right, and left us, but he still hovered around a few days, causing us to keep a sharp lookout for him; so if our numbers kept him away what difference does it make if our nerves were unstrung at the time. "All is well that end well."

That same afternoon, the Fiftieth Ohio was called into line, and marched to Camp King, back of Covington, going by way of a mud road that led east or rather southeast from our camp.

The writer was detailed to guard company goods, so remained in our first camp till the next day, when he rode in the wagon back through Covington, and so rejoined the company and regiment at Camp King. To the best of my recollection, we did not remain here but a few days, but quite long enough for some of our officers to have several more nervous attacks; the sight of two or three mounted men on some of the Licking Hills was sufficient excuse for them to have the regiment called out into line of battle.

Why, they seemed to think that the Confederates were planting batteries on all the hills that surround our camp; how it ever happened that such men as they got their commissions in the United States Volunteer Service has always been a puzzle to me.

My father and one of my brothers came to see me while at Camp King, and when I bade them good bye, that was the last I saw of any of my relatives until the close of the war. While on picket one day back of camp, I saw a razor back hog in the woods with a large knot on the end of its tail the size of my double fist. It was a freak of nature, and looked very odd to me. I wrote home to my people that the hogs were so poor out there that the owners had to tie knots in their tails to keep them from crawling through the fence cracks and straying away.

On the same post with me, a comrade after coming off of out post, rolled himself in his blanket, and laid down to take a little sleep. When we waked him in the morning, he got up and shook his blanket, and out rolled a large snake that had been his bed fellow. I imagine the comrade would not have slept very sound had he known of his snakeship sooner; as it was, that comrade jumped round there fully as lively as he would had the long roll [a long, continuous roll beat on the drum that was a signal to fall in under arms] been sounded, and I know it rattled him equally as bad. A day or two after this little incident, we received marching orders, and getting into line, we were soon on the move down through Covington.

Crossing the Licking Bridge, and passing through Newport, we bore to the right onto Saint John's Hill, and remained there one night, camping on the hillside in the rain. We passed a very disagreeable night; next day, we fell into line once more, and soon found ourselves marching out the Alexandria Pike, and in a short time, arrived at Camp Beechwood. I judge this was somewhere near where Fort Thomas now is, but of this, I am not positive. I remember very little of what took place in this

I will relate what I remember. We had a man in Company "K," who said his name was Thomas Easterling, yet I doubt very much if that was his right name. I judge he was a regular bounty jumper, for he never discarded his citizen's clothes, and finally deserted us while we were on the march to Perryville, Ky.

Bounty jumpers would enlist to collect the enlistment bounty and then desert to enlist at another location.—Ed. 2017

One day while lying in Camp Beechwood, two of the boys told Easterling that if he would go around a certain tent, there would be two white calves follow him. Easterling did not seem to pay much attention to them at first, but the boys kept on urging the matter, and seemed so anxious to get a bet out of him that the next day he told them to put up their money, and he would put up his; so the boys were so sure of their winning the money, they bet him $5.00, and both sides put up their money. Easterling marched around the tent, and then imagine their surprise, he pulled up his pants, and showed two black calves, following him instead of white ones; he had beat them at their own game by making liberal use of a box of shoe blacking. He won their money very easily, and after that, the boys were not so anxious to bet with Easterling.

Another incident I remember was a man that had one side of his head shaved, and drummed out of camp. I do not know what he had done, but I know I thought it was a very sad sight to look at. I remember nothing more of importance that occurred at this camp.

DRINKING FROM THE SAME CANTEEN

One morning after being in Camp Beechwood a few days, we received marching orders, and in a short time, we filed out of camp, and were soon tramping down the pike toward Newport and Covington, the boys, in high spirits, singing snatches of gay songs, such as "Ain't I glad to get out of the Wilderness," "Good bye, Mary Ann," and "The Girl I Left Behind Me."

Passing through Newport and Covington, we crossed the river on a pontoon bridge into Cincinnati, and marched down to the foot of Fifth street, and into the O. & M. Railroad Depot. Here a guard was thrown around us, with orders not to let any of us pass out, and we were told to make ourselves comfortable until morning, but what building was ever strong enough, or guards strict enough to hold strenuous Yankee soldiers in check, if they once took it in their heads to pass out; so, as it might be expected, a hole was soon found, and the boys were soon busy as bees, passing in and out, and like the bees, they all came in loaded; if not with honey, it was something that seemed to please the boys fully as well.

Next morning (Sunday I think), we were marched to one of the market houses, and breakfast was furnished us, and then we were returned to the depot, and put aboard the cars, and were soon steaming towards Jeffersonville, Indiana. The boys that were inclined to drink something stronger than coffee seemed to have plenty of it along, and as a result, there was ere long a very noisy, crowd aboard that train. Some were singing; some were talking and laughing; others whooping and yelling, and some were even crying, great tears rolling down their cheeks, and one German comrade had the misfortune of losing his hat, and created great amusement for us all, by exclaiming with a great deal of earnestness, "Sure, I had him all day, but now he is gone." Such was some of the different effects that drinking from the same canteen had on the boys that long to be remembered Sunday while on the way to Jeffersonville. Poor boys, many of them were never permitted to return, but their bones are crumbling to dust amid the soil of Kentucky, Tennessee and Georgia, while others are resting on the slimy bottom of the Mississippi River.

Arriving in Jeffersonville, we were ferried across the river into Louisville, and went into camp. You that are well versed in war history, will remember that at this time the Confederate General Bragg and the Federal General Buell were racing on parallel roads to see who would be the first to reach Louisville with his army, and remember also that General Buell won the race, and his coming was gladly welcomed by the loyal citizens of Louisville and the North. It was also an inspiration to us new troops to watch [Union General Don Carlos] Buell's dusty, sun-tanned and seasoned veterans proudly marching into Louisville, keeping perfect step to the inspiring music of their respective bands, and also to see the old flag floating proudly over them, the free breezes of Heaven kissing her beautiful folds, as she rippled, waved and glistened in the bright October sunshine. It was a grand and never-to-be-forgotten sight to us, and we hailed their coming with shouts of joy and thankfulness.

Buell's forces had been in the bloody fighting at Shiloh in April, 1862.— Ed. 2017

There was quite a contrast existing at that time between the clothing worn by Buell's men and that worn by our boys. Ours were new, and the "Sunday" was not worn off of them yet, while theirs were traveled stained, dusty and" appeared to have seen hard service, while the men were rugged and tanned, yet they carried themselves erect and seemed proud that it was their privilege to defend the flag under whose protecting folds they had been reared; so we found that under those soiled suits of blue were beating true and loyal hearts, ready and willing if need be to sacrifice their lives for that country and flag they loved so well, but the boys of the Fiftieth Ohio were soon to have the gloss taken off their clothes, and before many days our clothing looked fully as badly soiled as that of the boys marching with Buell.

We were not permitted to stop in Louisville any length of time, as our friends, the enemies under General [Braxton] Bragg, were still in the vicinity, so the Fiftieth took up the line of march with the balance of the army, and I want to tell the readers of this little story it was no picnic excursion marching over those hot, dusty roads after Bragg's army. That fall there had been a drought, and water was very hard to get, but dust was plentiful. This made it extremely hard on the men, especially new troops who were not used to marching. We all started out with well-filled knapsacks, but we did not get far before we trimmed ourselves down to light marching order; extra clothing was tossed aside to be gathered by the citizens or teamsters, for be it understood, we, had all drawn our full quota of clothing; every one of us had drawn an overcoat, something we had no need of that time of the year. Blistered feet were plentiful, and water being so hard to get, there was considerable suffering among the boys. I drank water on this march that the hogs had wallowed in; perhaps this sounds a little fishy or hoggish to some of you readers, but nevertheless, I will vouch for it being true. If you think this incident tough, let me give you another.

It was said that some of the boys got water out of a pond one dark night and used it at supper for to make their coffee, and to quench their thirst also. What was their disgust next morning to find a dead mule or two in the pond. I will not vouch for the truth of this, because it is a little too mulish but I have no doubt it was true. I imagine that coffee had a rich flavor.

But with all the unpleasantness of this short campaign, the boys tried to be cheerful, and would sing their little songs, and get off their little jokes on one another, and woe be to the one they got their jokes on; he better take it in good part, for if he got angry over it, he was not apt to hear the last of it for many a day. In a crowd of men and boys such as we were, there is always something more or less funny coming to the front to cause the laugh to go round, and so it was with us as we tramped along the dusty Kentucky roads leading to Perryville.

We had in Company "K," at that time, an old German comrade by the name of Bearman, a kind-hearted, generous old soul, who would willingly divide his last hardtack with a hungry comrade. He had seen hard service in his own country, but for some cause, he did not take kindly to our volunteer service, and found a great deal of fault with it. He was a short, heavy-set man, and carried a rather heavy knapsack; waddling along through the dust one day, comrade Bearman by some mischance, got' tangled up and fell on his back, his knapsack under him. fitted in a slight depression in the road made it a little difficult for him to get up in a hurry, and as we looked at him there on his back, his hands and feet fanning the air, he was such a comical sight. We greeted him with roars of laughter, and yelled at him to grab a root. Of course, this made him very angry, and when he finally got straightened up on his feet, he exclaimed passionately: "The longer a man lives, the more he finds by *Sheious* Christ out;" he was greeted by another roar of laughter from the boys, and for a short time, blistered feet and choking dust was forgotten, and whenever the boys would think how Bearman looked lying there in the dust, the laughter would burst out afresh; in fact, it was hard to forget the comical figure he cut while he was down; he reminded me very much of one of those large pinching bugs that we often see lying helpless on their backs in the dusty road. It was wrong perhaps to laugh at the old man, but in such cases the boys had no mercy on young or old, and poor Bearman was not suffered to forget this little mishap as long as he remained with us, but the service proved a little strenuous for such as he, and not long after this, he was given an honorable discharge, and sent home. The kindhearted old soul had taken a great liking to me, and gave me a very pressing invitation to come and see him after I got out of the service, promising me all the wine I could drink, as he said he had plenty of it in his cellar at home ,but I failed to pay him that visit, so missed getting the wine.

It was such amusing little incidents as this that kept the boys in good humor and spirits, and made them forget for the time being the hardships of the march.

Another thing that I noticed that always revived the drooping spirits of the boys, no matter how weary, footsore and thirsty they were, was for the band to strike up a spirited march, and the color bearer unfurl Old Glory to the breeze. Instantly the boys would straighten up their heads, grasp their muskets more firmly, step off more briskly, keeping perfect time to the tap of the drum, and even their faces would lighten up with pleasure. The sight of the old flag waving her graceful folds o'er their heads, and the lively music of the band, seemed to put new energy and new life in them, and someone perhaps more enthusiastic than the others would take off his cap, and swinging it in the air, would raise a cheer in which one by one the others would join till perhaps the whole regiment would be cheering. Other times someone of the boys would strike up that grand old song that we all loved so well: "Rally round the flag boys."

Comrade after comrade, and company after company would join in till hills and valleys would ring with the heart stirring chorines of the Union forever. "Hurrah, boys, hurrah! Down with the traitors, and up with the stars. Yes, well rally round the flag boys, rally once again, shouting the battle cry of freedom."

Such scenes and incidents as these were restful to the poor tired boys. It may seem strange to the reader who has never been a soldier, nevertheless, it is true, that whenever an old veteran catches sight of the old flag as she is unfurled to the breeze, and the sun begins to lighten up her beautiful colors of red, white and blue, that his pulse will beat faster, and his heart will begin to warm up, and he feels like he must shout, or that lump that is rising in his throat will choke him. Ah, yes! and I have seen them shed tears over it, and no wonder, for it represents all that is near and dear to them; take it away, and you take away their country, their home, aye their very life. Is it any wonder then that-they love it? "Long may it wave o'er the land of the free and the home of the brave." But let me get back, for I am digressing.

My memory does not serve me well enough to tell just how long it took us to march from Louisville to Perryville [over 300 miles; 480 km], but this much I do remember, it was very trying on new recruits. Both armies passing through the same section of country kept the wells and springs drained so dry it was almost impossible to get pure water, and some of the citizens, in fact, the majority of them had hid their well buckets and ropes, and we had nothing to draw with when we did reach a well where there was water. To make matters worse, our officers were very strict with the Fiftieth boys; they did not want us to leave the ranks to get water even when there was water to be got. They said they wanted no straggling. I suppose they were afraid the enemy would capture us.

I remember one night we camped not far from a little town, named Taylorsville, and it misted rain all night, and we had no tents, as this was before the pup tent came in style, at least with us. Laying out in the open air, our wool blankets absorbed all the rain that fell on them, and in the morning, they appeared to us as heavy as lead, and we were given no time to dry them, but were ordered to fall into line early, ready to resume the march, so the most of us left our blankets lay where they were, not knowing how far we would have to go that day, but the teamsters gathered them up, and put them in their wagons. We did not march more than two or three miles, and I think we were reviewed by some General Officer; if I knew who it was then, I have forgotten now.

We were marched up to the top of a high hill, overlooking the little town of Taylorsville, and camped there that day. The teamsters brought the blankets into camp, and spread them out to dry. I kept my eye on them, and as soon as they were dry enough, I took charge of one and rolled it up. That was the last blanket that I deliberately threw away, and had I known that we had such a short distance to march, I would have managed to carry it if it was water soaked, but as it turned out, I came out all right in the finish.

The reader will bear in mind that I am not trying to follow the movements of any other troops in this little story, except the Fiftieth Ohio, and only a mere sketch of them; in fact, it is more my own experience that I am trying to tell than anything else. True, I may weave into the story other comrades and other regiments, but in the main, I shall stick close to the Fiftieth, and especially Company "K" and myself.

Leaving Taylorsville, we again forged ahead on the road towards Perryville. On the evening of the 7th of October, 1862, the Fiftieth was late getting into camp, and the German element in Company "K" entertained us as we wearily marched along, with some of their choice German songs. After they grew tired, they were followed by a choir of American boys from Cincinnati. They sang us a little ditty about some little dog named Bingo. The song was said to contain one hundred verses, but they simply repeated the same verse over and over until I began, to think they would never run down, but about that time we filed off the road into camp, so that ended the concert for that evening, and before the next evening, we were to listen to another concert, quite different from this. It was by a full band, and was both instrumental and vocal with a deal of whistling in it.

Filing into camp, we stacked arms, unslung knapsacks, built fires, made coffee and after partaking of a hearty supper, of coffee, hardtack and bacon, we lay down, and rolling up in our blankets, our minds were soon revealing in the pleasant land of dreams.

BATTLE OF PERRYVILLE

The morning of the 8th of October was ushered in by the drummer boys beating the drums in the Union Camps; Bob Crandle doing his part by waking the Fiftieth Ohio boys from their pleasant sleep, and soon the delightful fragrance of boiling coffee and frying bacon permeated the fresh morning air. Hastily dispatching our breakfast, we were ordered into ranks, little dreaming that we were to run up against the business end of the "Johnnies" before nightfall.

Company "K" took her place in line, and once more the Fiftieth Ohio swung out into the dusty road with her flag proudly floating in the morning breeze, the boys stepping off with light hearts to the music of the band. The marching was not so hard on us now, as we were becoming more accustomed to it.

We were not long on the road till we began to hear the boom of cannon, or as some of the boys laughingly expressed it: "The bull dogs were beginning to bark." Presently we came in sight of the Signal Corps, busy at work, sending their messages to different parts of the field; batteries were hurrying past us, and we could see them as they went into battery on the nearby hills. Shells and solid shot began to drop uncomfortable near us, minnie balls would strike the ground with a dull thud near us, or go singing over our heads like bees on the wing. We were ordered to unsling knapsacks, and place them in a pile, and get ready for business. Again we move forward, and take our place in line of battle behind the Eightieth Indiana Regiment, who were supporting a battery, and are heavily engaged with the enemy. We are ordered to lie down in supporting distance, but the Indianans held their ground, and did not need our help though the Rebs made it hot for them.

I believe their loss was quite heavy. They were on higher ground than we were, and on the firing line. While we were in no great danger where we lay, yet I believe it was more trying on the nerves than being up in front, for the reason that we could do nothing where we were but lay and listened to the music, which appeared to be by the full band out in front, while the Indianans had a chance to get back at them, which I think was great satisfaction to them, at least, they seemed to take a lively interest in it.

I do not know how the other boys felt while we were lying there with the shot and shell and musket balls singing and whistling, o'er us, but I know I began to think we were up against the real thing this lime, and no mistake. No Fort Mitchell or Camp King, foolishness about this, and though there was a big dust arising out in front, it was not caused by a drove of government mules, but by real live Johnnie Rebs, very much alive too, from the way they sent their leaden and iron messages over among us; to say it was demoralizing would be putting it very mild indeed. I felt like there might be safer places to lie down than where we were just at that time. Perhaps, had I been given my choice just then, I would have preferred being back at Louisville or Cincinnati, but a soldier is given no choice in such small matters as these, but must try to do as he is ordered to do at all times.

In looking back over that trying time now, it all seems like a dream to me, and it is impossible for me to tell from memory at this late date all that I passed through on that never-to-be-forgotten day, and as I am now only writing from memory, if I should make mistakes or leave out some important moves that we made that day, I trust I may be excused by Comrades, who may chance to read this little narrative.

We were finally called up into line, and fell back behind a stone fence where we lay down again. We felt a little safer now, but were not permitted to stay here long, but were again called into line, and moved off by the left flank, and took positions on the firing line, on what seemed to me to be our extreme left flank. Here the Rebels in our front made it pretty warm for us, killing and wounding several in our regiment; among the number were three or four commissioned officers; two men were severely wounded in Company "K," a comrade on my left (my left bower, I called him) was struck by a bullet on the heel of his shoe, but was not otherwise hurt. I left my place in the ranks and advanced to an old log building out in our front, but as the bullets were singing around there pretty thick, I came back to the company again. There had been quite a number of men killed and wounded there from the way it looked to me, as the ground was covered with blood.

We held this place on the firing line until night, if I remember rightly, and then were moved a short distance to the rear, where we received a fresh supply of ammunition and the roll was called to see how many were missing. I think we passed the night here. I remember that all through the night I could hear the poor, wounded boys calling for water. The long dreary night came to an end at last, and we expected to be called on to renew the conflict, but when the day dawned, it was found that the enemy had silently stolen away. We suffered for water during the battle; it was very hard to get on our side; our Chaplain took as many canteens as he could carry, and rode off somewhere, and having filled them with water, returned them to us on the firing line, thereby gaining the admiration and respect of the boys for his fearlessness and bravery under fire.

The morning after the battle, a comrade and I took a number of canteens and went two miles, I would judge, towards our right flank before we found water enough to fill them. We found a spring, but the water ran very slow, and it took quite a while to get the canteens filled; while there, we heard the cavalry out farther on our right flank and front, having quite a lively skirmish. The cracking of the carbines reminded me of the popping of fire crackers under a barrel, only the reports were much louder. The comrade and I did not spend any more time than was necessary at the spring, for that firing was too close for us to feel safe, and we thought the last canteen was a long time filling; however, it was full at last, and we were not sorry when we got started on our return to camp. When we had covered about half the distance to camp, we came on some comrades that had slaughtered a hog, and they kindly offered us a share, which we gladly accepted, and we hastily laid aside our canteens, and were soon busy cooking and eating fresh meat. After satisfying our hunger, we once more gathered up our canteens and struck out for camp, and to our dismay when we reached it, we found the regiment had moved, and it was sometime before we could locate them, but at last we found them camped on a ridge, near a creek, in which there was a few pools of water, but by night they were drained so low that

I caught a few small fish with my hands and cleaned them and had fish for my supper. I will say here we never got our knapsacks anymore. Some of the boys went back where we left them the day after the battle and found them all cut to pieces and the contents mostly carried off or destroyed.

The reader will observe that the Fiftieth Ohio was not very deep in the trouble at Perryville, though I must say we did all we were called on to do, and that I believe is all that is required of a good soldier. The regiment at that time were armed with old Australian rifles, and quite a number of them would not burst a cap, only about every third trial, so I think it is well we did not get in the thick of it.

I believe there was some dissatisfaction with General Buell at that time by the Administration at Washington, in regard to his conduct relating to the Battle of Perryville. If I mistake not, the General denied having any knowledge of a general engagement till too late to send reinforcements. While this may be true, yet if he was anywhere in hearing that day, he must have thought the, boys were having a pretty big skirmish, but many queer things happen during the war, and letting a few men fight the Battle of Perryville, while hundreds lay in camp in hearing distance that would have been glad to have taken a part, is one of them.

Many rumors were afloat in our camp at that time; among them was the one that General Bragg and General Buell were brothers-in-law, and that they had eaten supper together the night before the battle. I give these rumors for what they are worth, not knowing whether they are true or false.

False. Perryville was tactically indecisive but caused Bragg's withdrawal; Buell was severely criticized for not aggressively pursuing Bragg. He was relieved of command.—Ed. 2017

Before leaving Cincinnati, I had been given a fifty dollar check for my Hamilton County local bounty, and having some trouble in getting mail to and from home, I still had the check with me at Perryville. A day or two after the battle, my Lieutenant came to me and inquired if I still had that check with me. I said I had, and told him the reason I had not sent it home. "Well," said he, "Mr.—

(naming a gentleman that had come with us from Cincinnati) is going back to his home, and all letters given to him, he will mail either at Louisville or Cincinnati." So he advised me to send my check by him. I thought myself that would be a good plan, so I wrote a letter, and placing my check in it, sealed and addressed it to my father at Covington, Kentucky, and that was the last I ever heard of my check. My father never received it, but after the close of the war, by the help of General Strickland, I succeeded in collecting my fifty dollars from the Hamilton County Commissioners, but what ever became of the check is still a mystery to me.

I also had three dollars in silver in my pocket at Perryville, but after spending that, it was many a long day before I saw any more silver money.

I cannot say just how long we remained near the battle ground.

I think, perhaps, the third day after the fight we moved our camp to a large, spring of water. It had a building over it, and I think it was as fine a spring as ever I saw. There was no lack of water there for both man and beast; that was one great advantage the Rebels had over us at Perryville. They had plenty of water behind them, while we had to suffer for the want of it.

The army under General Buell pressed on after the Rebel army, the Fiftieth Ohio going as far as Crab Orchard. I remember of passing through Danville on the way.

After getting to Crab Orchard, the Fiftieth Ohio was ordered back to Lebanon, Kentucky. The nights were beginning to be cold now, and we began to miss our blankets and overcoats, which we lost at Perryville. Our shoes were beginning to wear out also, and we were getting short of clothing all around. Before we got to Lebanon, there came a fall of snow and as we had no tents, we had to make shelter out of rails and straw or whatever we could get hold of that would answer that purpose.

Taking all these things into consideration, we began to think soldiering was not the most pleasant life that one could desire, but as we knew we were in for it, good or bad, the most of us took the matter in a sensible way, and tried to get all the good out of it we could. Of course, we had a few that would complain, for you know some men would even grumble if they were going to be hung.

We reached Lebanon sometime the last of October. Here we drew tents and clothing, which we needed badly enough. The weather had now become quite wintry, and the boys had fine sport killing rabbits, which were plentiful in the fields around Lebanon.

Jack Walters, a member of Company had the misfortune of getting a musket ball through his right index finger. That ended his rabbit hunting for a short time; he afterwards deserted us, and went home; was arrested, and put to work on fortifications somewhere, and took sick and died, so it was reported to us. Poor Jack, he was a good-hearted boy, but he got tired of the army, got homesick and this in the end caused his death.

One of the commissioned officers of the Fiftieth that was wounded at Perryville died at Springfield among some of his relatives, while we were at Lebanon and there was a detail of a hundred men taken out of the Fiftieth to go out and bury him with the honors of war. The writer was one of the detail. We were all furnished a pair of white gloves and made quite a nice appearance. When we returned to the house from the graveyard we were given a fine lunch. Springfield is not far from Lebanon. We rode out and back in army wagons.

Having got tired carrying a gun that was so uncertain about going off, I traded for a Belgium rifle. It was sure fire, and the boys called it a young cannon. Well, it surely did roar when it went off, and it was about as dangerous to stand behind it as it was to stand in the front of it. I called it "Old never fail."

About the 13th of November, we were ordered to Columbia, a small town forty miles from Lebanon. A good turnpike led from Lebanon to Columbia. We passed through Newmarket and Campbellsville on our way. Campbellsville was just about half way between the two places.

Our camp at Columbia was very unhealthy. The Eightieth Indiana was camped here with us. Both regiments had considerable sickness and some deaths. Colonel Taylor, having left us at Perryville,

Strickland was now promoted to Colonel and had command of the regiment. Captain Cook was promoted to Lieutenant Colonel, and Major Defrees having resigned, Elsner was promoted to Major, and Jerome F. Crawley to Adjutant.

We arrived at Columbia the 15th of November and remained here drilling and doing guard duty till December 22nd.

AFTER JOHN MORGAN

John Morgan was now in Kentucky on one of his many raids, and was threatening the town of Lebanon and we were ordered back there.

John Hunt Morgan (1825–1864) had led his rebel forces on a costly raid in Kentucky, which was part of the encouragement to send Bragg into the state. He was later killed during a raid on Greeneville, TN.—Ed. 2017

Leaving Columbia, December 22nd, we marched back to Lebanon, Morgan being out about Springfield at this time. I think we must have spent our Christmas at Lebanon, but am not positive.

Morgan hovered around near us till the last day of December, when he circled around us and started for Columbia. We were started out after him, taking the pike towards Newmarket, Campbellsville and Columbia. Morgan succeeded in reaching Newmarket ahead of us, and some Colonel out of a Kentucky regiment that was with us getting too far in advance ran into Morgan's rear guard and was killed by them. We were thrown into line of battle at Newmarket just about dark New Years' Eve, with strict orders to build no fires and keep our accouterments on and sleep if we could for the cold with our muskets by our sides. As might be expected, we passed a very disagreeable night, as the weather was cold and frosty. I could hear the boys knocking their shoes together all night trying to keep their feet warm. All remained quiet in our front during the night. There was a rail fence in front of us and as the first faint rays of daylight tinged the eastern sky we were roused up, ordered to stack arms and take the top rails of that fence and make fires and get our breakfast as quick as we could. Wishing each other a happy New Year we charged that fence without a break in the line, taking the top rails as ordered and soon had a line of fires reaching from one end of our line of battle to the other.

We were not long in cooking and dispatching our breakfast, consisting of coffee, hardtack and fat bacon. The bugle sounded fall in and once, more we took up the line of march after Morgan. The pike after leaving Newmarket led up over quite a high hill; a strong position for the enemy had he been disposed to resist our advance and many of us supposed that Morgan would show us battle here, as he could have placed his artillery in the pike on the hill, and held us in check with a very small force, but it seems he had made no stop here longer than to destroy the telegraph line. We had with us several post teams; they were brought up now, and each wagon was loaded with men, and the mules put on the jump, so it was Yankee infantry on wheels now after Morgan's Rebel Cavalry. The drivers did not appear to have very much control over their six mule teams; if they kept the middle of the pike, well and good; there were some very narrow places in the pike and my hair stood on end several times for fear we would upset and roll down the bank, but fortunately there was no accident of that kind happened that I heard of.

We now began to see plenty of broken down horses and mules that had been turned adrift by Morgan in his flight. Citizens told us that he was making fast time. Passing through Campbellsville, he captured a lot of commissary stores; took what they could carry and tried to destroy the balance. He also captured and paroled a few sick men that were there in the hospital. But now we are nearing Green River on the south side of which is another hill like the one at New Market, and also a partially completed block house, which we were working on when we received orders to go to Lebanon. Now we thought surely if Morgan wants to fight he has the drop on us and as if to convince us that we are correct this time, the wagons are halted. We are ordered to get out and move to one side to let our battery pass, which has been in the rear; they pass us on the trot, and we soon hear them in action up in front. After a few rounds, they cease firing, and we move on to the river, only to find that Morgan has passed over, and burnt the bridge, and also a large amount of corn that was cribbed up here. Our battery had only fired a few rounds at his rear guard that they saw fast disappearing on the opposite side of the river. There had been a large amount of corn stored here in rail pens that had been raised on the Green River bottoms, but this was now fast turning to ashes and the heat from the burning corn was so great that the boys could not approach it close enough to light their pipes.

Morgan did not take advantage of the unfinished fort on Green River hill, but pushed on toward Columbia.

We were forced to ford the river in wagons, near the smoking ruins of the bridge, and continued the pursuit, passing more abandoned horses and mules on the way.

Citizens told us that Morgan seemed to be in a great hurry to reach Columbia; as we neared the town, we heard musketry, and I began to think there was a skirmish on hand, but when we got close enough to see what the firing meant I saw it was some of the boys in advance, killing hogs, and that too while the owners were trying to drive them where they could care for them. Thus ended our New Year's ride, 1863, after General John Morgan's Rebel Cavalry.

It was now plain to us why Morgan did not offer us battle at Newmarket or Green River bridge—the Union Cavalry under Woolford was coming in on another road, trying to head him off at Columbia, which they would have done had he halted at either place to dispute our passage. Morgan understood this, I suppose from his scouts, hence his great haste to get past Columbia. As it was, Morgan's rear guard left the town just about one-half hour before Wool ford's advance struck it. The infantry were halted now, and the cavalry took up the pursuit, running Morgan out of the state. I heard the artillery giving them a few parting shots at the Cumberland River, as Morgan passed out of sight into Tennessee. I will just say here that Morgan's forces were defeated at this crossing of Green River by a small force of Federals, when he started on his celebrated raid into Ohio the following summer [June 11–July 26, 1863].

We remained at Columbia till the 4th of January. While there, I was placed on camp guard and there came a heavy rainstorm; there was no shelter and after I had got thoroughly wet, the word was passed round for the guards to go to quarters; the result was I took a heavy cold and had a bad bilious attack. I went to the doctor and he gave me three powders; I downed one of them, but it would not stay down; the other two, I threw down in the bushes. I don't know whether they stayed down or not, as I never went to look after them.

On the evening of the 3rd, we received orders to be ready to march at daylight in the morning. I was feeling pretty bad, so I got my knapsack in a wagon and Lieutenant Pine and Sergeant Kelso took turns in carrying "Old never fail," so I fared pretty well, and arrived in camp at Campbellsville that evening with the company; after a good night's rest, I felt a great deal better. We rested at Campbellsville two days, and then we were ordered to New Haven, Kentucky, which place we reached January 10th. This was a hard march for us, nothing but clay roads to march over, and it seemed to us as if there was no bottom to them. Talk about your mud. You that have traveled over Kentucky clay roads in the winter season can form some idea what a picnic we had. To make matters worse, I think the guide was lost a good portion of the time. The teams started from Campbellsville with us with plenty of rations, but we left them so far in the rear that we never saw them anymore till a day or two after we arrived in New Haven. They stuck in the mud soon after starting out, and as fast as they would pull out of one bad place they would hang up in another, until finally when they did get up with us there was not much left in the wagons. I presume the teamsters threw away nearly all their loads and were glad to get through with their empty wagons and mules. The result of this mismanagement was that when the third morning dawned on us we had nothing to eat. I remember distinctly that all I had for breakfast was a small piece of corn bread, perhaps an inch and a half square, and two or three swallows of cold coffee, but when the order was given to fall in Company "K," I shortened my belt and took my place on the right of the company, and kept it all day; at dinner, I shortened my belt two or three more holes and determinedly, if not cheerfully, marched along. I never saw as much straggling before or afterwards in the regiment as was done that day. The boys took in both flanks for miles foraging for something to eat. When we struck camp that evening, there was just enough men left in old Company "K" to make one stack of guns, and the writer was one among that lucky number; though, needless to say, he had taken up his belt to the last hole before he arrived there, but it still had considerable slack in it.

Joseph Stagmire, a German comrade of Company "K," and I had made an agreement together as we marched along that we would remain with the Company till we reached camp, and then we would do a little foraging for ourselves in a private way. As soon then as we had received orders to break ranks, we laid aside our knapsacks and accouterments, and started for the first house we could see; arriving there, the gentleman of the house informed us that his folks all had the measles, and that it was impossible for them to get us anything to eat; (quite likely this was only a bluff) I asked him if he could direct us anywhere that he thought it was likely we could get something to eat, as we had had nothing all day, and were very hungry. Said he, "If you'ns will follow that road there through that piece of woods, it will lead you out among some pretty well-to-do farmers that I think will give you'ns all something to eat." We thanked him, and took the road (a bridle path) he had pointed out; it began to be quite dark by this time, and we had some trouble in keeping the path; however, after going about a mile, we saw a light glimmering in the distance. Needless to say, we hastened to it. Just about the same time that we knocked at the back door, three other comrades knocked at the front door. In answer to our knock, a lady came to the door. I made known to her our wants and told her we had no money to pay her for the trouble nor the food.

She answered that that was all right; that they were going to get supper for those other three men that had come in the other way, and that it would not be much more trouble to cook for five than it would for three. She invited us in a room where there was a large fire place with a pleasant fire burning in it, before which we seated ourselves, and enjoyed its homelike comfort while the ladies of the house prepared supper. The man of the house seemed to be a perfect gentleman and a strong Union man, and I have no doubt he was, as the whole family treated us royally. Soon the ladies announced that supper was ready, and such a supper as that was. kind reader, it had not been our fortune to see since leaving home. There were spare ribs, backbone, sausage, warm biscuits and Sutter; coffee and milk and pie, besides other things that went to make that supper one long to be remembered, and it is useless for me to say that us five poor,' hungry soldier boys did ourselves proud in stowing it away. If I had been wearing my belt then I am satisfied I would have been compelled to let it out full length, showing that one extreme follows another.

The gentleman gave us a pressing invitation to stay all night with them, but, of course, we did not feel at liberty to accept, so after warming and resting awhile longer by the fire, we took our leave, but not before expressing to them our sincere and heartfelt thanks for their kindness. Poor comrade Stagmire! how he did enjoy that supper; he often spoke to me about it afterwards, and he and I made a vow that if we ever got near them again, we would certainly go and pay for that supper, but we were never permitted what would have been to us a great pleasure. The family lived quite close to what was then called Camp Wickliffe, but I am sorry that I have entirely forgotten their names. I see in a letter that I wrote my mother from New Haven two or three days after this that I told her about that supper, but I did not tell her how hungry I was before I got it.

I always tried to present the bright side of everything when I wrote home while in the service, and always tried to appear cheerful and happy, but I suppose the most of the boys did that way that had any love and respect for their relatives.

When Stagmire and I arrived in camp, we found that most of the stragglers had come in and from the busy way that we saw them employed about the camp fires, showed us they had been very successful in foraging off of the country that day. My messmates just had supper ready, consisting of chicken soup, flapjacks and molasses, and, well, I ought to be ashamed to tell it, but I positively sat down and ate another supper, and reader you could not have told had you been watching me that it was the second time that I had been there that evening. After satisfying my hunger the second time, I laid down, rolled up in my blanket, and I think

I can say in all candor that if I did not sleep sound that night it was not for the want of something to eat.

The next day we marched to New Haven, arriving there about 2 o'clock; this was on either the 9th or 10th of January. We remained here about two weeks; during that time, we had a very heavy fall of snow. It fell in the night, and in the morning we could scarcely get out of our pup tents for it. There was nothing of importance transpired at this place while we were there I had another slight sick spell while here, and the boys taught me to play cards while lying in our tents to pass away the time.

Sergeant Kelso and Sergeant Lousy [Losey] went to the sutlers one night and bought some wine and other knickknacks, and knowing I was not feeling very well, they called me to their tent and treated me. It was very kind in them to do so, and I always had a warm corner in my heart for the two sergeants afterwards. Their treat brought me around all right, and in a day or two I was ready for duty once more.

About the 22nd or 23rd we were put aboard the cars and sent to Louisville.

The following little incident happened while we were all busy loading our goods on the train ready to ship to Louisville. It seemed as though there had been a Negro who gave his master the slip and joined himself to our regiment, but his master had got on his trail and traced him to our camp. Colonel Strickland was on his iron gray horse earnestly engaged superintending the loading of the cars, when the irate master of the said contraband approached him, and in an angry voice demanded his "nigger.' Colonel Strickland told him he did not want his "nigger," and knew nothing about him, but still the master kept following the Colonel, demanding his "nigger." Said he, "You'ns all stole my nigger, and I want you'ns all to give him up." This made Colonel Strickland angry, and he pulled out his revolver and pointing it at the man he said, "Now, sir, I want you to quit bothering me, or I will let daylight through you. I don't care anything about you or your damn nigger." This closed the incident, and the master went without his "nigger."

It's surprising how many veterans told a similar tale of slaveholders asking Union commanders to relinquish escaped slaves. The escaped African-Americans were designated "contraband of war" by the Union and therefore they refused to return them. This was shortened and often, Blacks were just referred to as "contrabands."—Ed. 2017

We remained in camp at Louisville until about the first of February, when we were sent out by rail to Muldraugh's Hill to guard trestles on the Louisville and Nashville Railroad, 36 miles from Louisville.

CAMP LIFE

Arriving at Muldraugh's Hill, the Fiftieth Ohio was divided as follows: One company was placed at Salt River Bridge for guard duty, and the balance of the regiment was divided into two battalions; the first battalion, in charge of Colonel Strickland, was placed at Little Run trestle; the second battalion, in charge of Elsner, who had now been promoted to Lieutenant Colonel (Cook having resigned), was placed at Big Run trestle to do guard duty at those places.

John Morgan had recently captured the troops that were here, and burnt the trestles, but they had now been rebuilt and trains were again running on time.

When we first arrived here in the beginning of February, we found it pretty cold and dreary, but we went bravely to work and soon had very snug quarters put up, and when the weather got fine we had beautiful camps for each battalion. We fortified each camp pretty strongly and prepared to give the "Johnnies" a warm reception had they been disposed to visit us.

The writer had now been promoted to Corporal, and had charge of one of the guns in the fort, and took daily lessons in artillery drill. It cost us quite an amount of labor to prepare our camps and to fortify them, but we felt amply repaid when the bright, warm spring arrived and arrayed the surrounding forest in her beautiful dress of green, and the wild flowers beneath the spreading branches of the trees burst into bloom, filling the soft spring air with their sweet fragrance. The feathered songsters also did their part to enliven the scene, filling the woods with their happy songs of praise to the Great Creator of the Universe.

Yes, the Fiftieth Ohio was now at home, eating their white bread, and knowing this, we boys made the most of it. We enjoyed ourselves as only soldiers can when not on duty. I can assure you that the fun in camp was fast and furious, playing cards, fiddling and dancing, singing songs, writing letters ,to our sweethearts and friends, jumping matches, pitching quoits, and last, but not least, teasing and playing jokes on each other.

We formed the acquaintance of citizens for miles outside of camp in the surrounding country, and at their dances would keep them up to the wee small hours of the morning, and in this way, they appeared to enjoy themselves immensely, but very few accidents happened that I remember to mar the pleasure of the boys while encamped here.

An officer was cleaning his revolver one day when it was accidentally discharged, shooting him in the foot, but not serious. One or two of the boys were shot also while fooling with their revolvers, but none of the accidents were serious that I can call to mind.

Quite a number of the boys' relatives came to see them here this summer. There were no furloughs given at this time, but some of the boys took French leave and came home while others got passes. My company officers wrote me a pass and signed it and I took it to Colonel Strickland for his signature, but he says to me, "My boy, you will have to wait till some of the others return, there are too many away now." But I never got home on that pass. I was disappointed, but had to make the best of it.

Captain Hendricks resigned while here, and First Lieutenant McClure was promoted to Captain. Second Lieutenant Pine was promoted to First Lieutenant, and Orderly Sergeant C. A. Vandaurson to Second Lieutenant, and John Lindsey to Orderly Sergeant.

Some very amusing things happened while we remained in this camp, but I cannot recall many of them at this late date. Sergeant Lousey bought a bottle of brandy peaches from our sutler one day because he got them cheap, and he treated me to some of the brandy, and also the peaches; then he got away with what was left, which was a little more than he bargained for. Lousey was a man that was not in the habit of indulging in anything as strong as brandy peaches, so the result was Lousey got funny, and when I say "funny," that is exactly what I mean, for all that poor Lousey could do was to sit on his bunk and laugh. In the midst of his hilarity, who should step in but Captain Hendricks, and I think he must have been eating brandy peaches also, or something fully as strong, for the monkey shines that those two cut in that tent was equal to any circus Lever saw. They both seemed to realize the moment they saw each other's eyes the fix they were both in, and for a half hour or more they sat there and laughed at each other; they did no harm, but simply laughed. But finally the brandy began to die away and then Lousey got sick. He got out of his tent, and made his way to a small tree and laid down in the shade, and a sicker man I never saw. If it could have been possible, I think he would have thrown up the soles of his shoes. This was the last and only time that I ever knew Sergeant Lousey to put an enemy in his mouth to steal away his brains during our term of service.

The boys used to have a good deal of sport at my expense. I was the tallest man in the company, measuring six feet and three inches; it so happened that it got to be a common thing for it to rain whenever I went on picket, so when the boys would see me start out, they would say, "Well, boys, we may look for rain today, for there goes Winters on picket, and he will be sure to stir up the clouds with his head," and whether I did disturb the clouds or not, it seemed that their predictions that it would rain most always proved true.

One day during the early days of summer, I felt something crawling up my backbone; it would stop at short intervals, long enough to take a bite or two, and then do some more crawling. My curiosity was aroused; I slipped out in the bushes and pulled off my shirt and turning it inside out, began to scrutinize it pretty close, and what is this I have found? O misery of miseries! five or six gray backs [lice]; I had heard of the beasts, but this was my first introduction to them and I thought I was ruined for life. It was a very crestfallen boy that made his way back into camp, and to say that my nervous system was shocked is putting it mild indeed. In a year or so after this, they became our closest companions, and we could not sleep sound unless we had three or four teams of them playing football and catcher on our body.

Growing tired of the monotony of camp, and wishing for a change of scene, Comrade Henry Liebrook and I, one evening after roll call, decided to call on some young ladies that lived very near one of our picket post. So after paying a visit to our sutler and fortifying the inner man with a few bottles of ginger wine, we very slyly, as we thought, stole our way out of camp, but the sequel will show that there were others as sly as we were, and stood ready to take up our trail with the cunning of a pack of fox hounds. To avoid our guards and pickets, we gave all the roads, and paths a wide berth, and pushed our way through the thickets and tangled underbrush of the virgin forest that lay between us and our destination. The owls perched in the tree-tops above our heads, gazed down in astonishment at the two boys in blue intruding upon their grounds, and with solemn voices inquired, "Who are you?" And the whippoorwills (and by the way there seemed to be hundreds of them), were making all kinds of threats to "Whip Will," but we paid no heed to these questions or threats, but pushed steadily on, and in due time arrived safe at the house where we found the ladies and also another comrade, who I suppose had grown tired of camp also, and had gotten there before us, but this did not worry me. I forthwith began to make myself agreeable to one of the young ladies, and I was succeeding to my entire satisfaction, when in stepped three other comrades, that had trailed Liebrook and me, and run us to cover. This was just a little more than we bargained for. However, someone proposed we have a game of cards. Two decks were produced and comrade John Klotter and I chose the ladies as our partners, took seats at one table and started a game of "Seven-up," while the other four comrades commenced a game of euchre on another table, and for a short time the fun in that room bordered on what might be termed fast and furious. My lady partner and I were simply having it all our own way with our opponents, but the euchre players got too noisy, and their loud thumps on the table with their trumps reached the ears of the officer at the picket post, and he sent over a file of men and put us all under arrest and marched us over to the reserve, where it was found that comrade Liebrook had given the guards the slip, and had dodged into the bushes and made tracks for camp. The officers, after holding us at the reserve for ten or fifteen minutes, told us to go to camp and behave ourselves, which we at once proceeded to do. I found comrade Liebrook in the tent, rolled up in his blanket. He had had his change of scene and was satisfied.

This was the first, last and only time I was ever put under arrest while in the service by Uncle Sam's officers.

Later on, I was placed under arrest by a big Johnnie Rebel, but of that, I will tell about hereafter. I would not have the reader get the impression that I never did anything to be arrested for by no means, but there is an old saying that seems to fit in my case, and that is: "Catching before hanging always." True, I was of a quiet, reserved disposition, but there is another saying that might have been applied here in regard to myself, and that is: "Still water runs deep." But I did but very little grumbling, and was always ready for duty, whatever it might be. Still, I think, had the officers been close observers, they might have seen my face flush up very red when they gave me the cognomen of "Old honest Winters." I fear I did not always deserve to be so honored.

Among my comrades in Company "K" was Steven D. Blizzard, a tall, raw-boned Virginian, dark complected, with black, curly hair, and whiskers slightly streaked with grey.

He was a married man, and as he could not write, he often had me to write letters for him to his wife at home, and he used to often say with a laugh, when the weather was cold and stormy, that he wished he was home with Nancy. He was a brave and fearless soldier, and under his suit of blue, beat a true and kindly heart. He was always ready to go where duty called him, and always ready and willing to help a deserving comrade out of trouble. He was a whole-souled, generous comrade, ever willing to lend a helping hand in any innocent sport among the boys, and quick to resist an insult, or to take the part of a comrade that he thought was being imposed on. No one enjoyed a good joke or story better than himself, and he seemed to have a peculiar knack of telling a story or joke to make it interesting and enjoyable.

He used to relate a joke on himself that he enjoyed very much. We had a comrade in Company "K" that got a little homesick, and whenever we would draw our pay, that comrade would get on a spree, and run through with all his money, trying to drown his troubles in drink. Blizzard, thinking to save some of the comrade's money, and at the same time keep the comrade sober, borrowed fifteen or twenty dollars from him, with the intention, of course, to save it for the comrade, but alas! what did Blizzard do but blow the money in himself. I have heard him relate this, and laugh over it heartily many a time.

Blizzard and I were very good friends, and one day we got a pass and took a stroll out in the country. The pass was limited to so many hours, but we became so much interested in the company we met, we took no note of time, and when we arrived in sight of camp, the sun was fast disappearing behind the western hills. As soon as the boys caught sight of us, they began to yell at us, and tell us we were blacklisted; we would get no more passes. We answered them that was all right, for we knew we deserved it, as we had overstayed our pass, but in two or three days after this, as Blizzard and I came off of picket one morning, we decided to ask for another pass, not that we wanted it, or expected to get it, but merely to see what our officers had to say to us about our other pass. Blizzard said he would ask for the pass; so after washing himself, he went up to company headquarters, combing his hair and whiskers.

Lieutenant Vandourson was in command of Company "K" at that time. Blizzard stepped into the tent, and greeted the Lieutenant very pleasantly, and said, "Lieutenant, will you give Winters and me a pass this morning?" Vandourson looked up with a terrible frown on his face, and answered, "I gave you and Winters a pass the other day, and you went off and never came back." Blizzard stood and looked at him a while, and said, "How in the hell would we be here now if we never came back?" This was too much for Vandourson; the frown disappeared from his face, and breaking out into a hearty laugh, he proceeded to write the pass.

Comrade Coleman Quinn and I were taking a walk on the railroad one day when I had the good fortune to find a beautiful silver-mounted revolver that belonged to Lieutenant Crowley. The officer gave me a two dollar bill on some Ohio bank as a reward for returning his revolver. The bill was O. K. at that time, but that was the last old Ohio money that I ever saw. Greenbacks came into circulation then, and all other money was swept out of sight.

Comrade John F. Heberlein, my left bower, and I got permission one day to visit the railroad tunnel a mile or so above camp. While there, we called at a citizen's house nearby, who kept whiskey, the regular old white rifle kind, warranted to kill at a hundred yards. Now whether Heberlein indulged in it more freely than I, or whether I could stand more than him, is a question I am not able to answer at this late date, but be that as it may, when we got back to the trestle, Heberlein's head was a great deal too heavy for the rest of his body to support, and his legs would get badly tangled up at times, but yet when he came to the trestle, he swore he was going to cross it. Now the said trestle was between us and camp, and was one hundred feet from the earth at the highest point, with a single plank, perhaps six inches wide running between the tracks, and it took a man with steady nerves to walk it at any time. In his condition, I knew, he would fall to his death; he was very determined, and wanted to try it, but by hard coaxing, I finally persuaded him to go down underneath, and so we reached camp by that route, Heberlein howling and yelling like a wild Indian on the war path all the while. I felt very much ashamed of my left bower at the time, and slipped into my tent out of sight as quickly as possible. Such little incidents as those kept us in good spirits, and I may say we were a jolly set of boys, while guarding the railroad trestles at Muldraugh's Hill.

A SMALL REBEL RAID

Just under the hill below our camp was quite a village of Irish people living; the men worked on the railroad; some of the women kept whiskey to sell; among them, a Mrs. Casey. The boys that felt disposed, therefore, did not have far to go after their morning dram; if they had stopped at one dram, it would not have been so bad, but some of the boys never knew when to stop, as long as they had any money, and this caused matters to move pretty lively in camp at times, showing that the man who wrote that "Drinking is the soldier's pleasure," was not far from wrong. It is a singular fact, but there are some men who would go through fire and water for a little whiskey; as for myself, I never loved it well enough to make much of a sacrifice to obtain it. I am very thankful that I never cultivated a taste for it.

Elizabethtown was situated about four miles from Big Run trestle, where the second battalion was camped.

Comrade John Bennett and I left camp one morning without any pass, and without asking any leave, and went to Elizabethtown, and spent the day. We had a jolly good time, but our officers gave us a pretty good talking to for it. We had come off of picket that morning, and were excused from duty for the day, or I think they would have given us a little taste of double duty.

I here make a few extracts from letters sent home to my parents, brothers and sisters from this camp.

Under date of February 6th, I wrote:

"We are now camped on the Louisville and Nashville Railroad, 36 miles from Louisville, guarding some trestles that John Morgan burned in one of his raids through Kentucky.

"The trestles have been rebuilt and trains are making their regular trips. Morgan captured the troops that were here before us, after an hour's engagement, they having no artillery, while Morgan had several pieces with him. We have now five pieces of artillery here, and are learning to manage them ourselves, for in case of an attack, we will have to handle the guns, as there are no artillery men here.

"I am in excellent health-and spirits."

Writing to my brother under date of February 13th:

"I received my boots and the money you sent me, through the kindness of Mr. Vanosdol. Many thanks. Am well pleased with my boots, though they are a trifle large. I will try to fill them as you wish, but I cannot fill them with my feet. They will do me a great deal of good this spring, during the wet weather.

"Would love to see you all, but would not be satisfied to stay at home as long as the Union is threatened, and the old flag in danger.

"Regiment after regiment are being shipped down the road to Nashville. Expect to hear of some hard fighting being done there ere long."

Writing to my sister under date of February 16th, I say:

"I was made very happy to hear from you all once more, and know you were all well, and enjoying the smiles of God's providence.

"This is a fine day, the sun is shining in all its beauty and splendor; the camp is full of merriment, for this is pay day and that makes us all happy.

"You write you heard I was the stoutest man in the regiment; that is partially true. I am enjoying the best of health, and weigh 180 pounds, but I do not claim to be the stoutest man in the regiment. If all goes well, I might enjoy that distinction in the near future."

February 17th, to my mother, I say:

"We have received our pay, and we all have our pockets full of greenbacks.

"Dear Mother, pray for me that God may bring me safe home to join the happy family circle once more. May a Heavenly Father's choicest blessings rest on you all is the earnest prayer of your soldier son."

Under date of February 24th, write to brother that:

"There is a rumor in camp that the Rebels have entered Kentucky again, six thousand strong, and are marching toward this railroad in order to cut off Gen. [William] Rosecrans' supplies.

"We are looking for an attack here in a few days. For fear there might be truth in the rumor, we are expressing all our spare cash home. If they do attack us, we will give them the best we got in the shop."

Under date of March 12th, writing to a sister in Ohio, I state:

"We are having fine weather, and work four hours a day fortifying our camps.

"Think we will remain here for some time. We have nice comfortable camps here, and for soldiers, we are having good times.

"I suppose there is great excitement out your way on account of the draft. Well, I am glad that I volunteered, and if it is God's will that I should get home safe, I shall never regret that I came out to help defend Old Glory."

March 24th, in answer to a letter received from my parents, through the kindness of comrade Childs, I tell them how glad I am to hear that they are in good health, and enjoying the smiles of Providence.

"Pen cannot portray the joy and happiness it affords me to get a letter from those I love; from those who nursed me, fed and clothed me, watched over and protected me from harm in childhood and youth; whose prayers I know now daily ascend to a throne of grace, asking the Heavenly Father to protect the one whose chair is vacant in the family circle.

"May God bless and prosper and keep you from all the evils that are in the world, is the humble prayer of your grateful son.

"I am still in good health and getting along as well as could be expected, seeing that I am surrounded by so many alluring temptations incident to a soldier in camp, as we are here.

"We have our camps nearly surrounded by rifle pits and other strong works of defence. We keep out a force of pickets and if they do their duty it would seem almost impossible for an enemy to take us by surprise. However, I do not think we will ever be attacked at this point."

March 27th and 30th:

"There has been quite an excitement in camp for a few days, owing to a report that the Rebels were in Kentucky again in pretty strong force. Well, if they pay us a visit they will find us at home."

April 17th, 18th and 19th:

"All quiet at Muldraugh's Hill. We have a beautiful place for camps here; it is high and dry. We have our quarters all sided up with slabs, and use our tents for the roof; this makes them more roomy and healthy.

"The regiment is enjoying the best of health. We are having fine weather here; the warm sun almost gives us the spring fever, I have not heard any news lately concerning the armies at Vicksburg, and Charleston. I hope our armies will keep crowding the rebs, until the old flag shall again proudly float over every town and hamlet in Dixie. May God speed the day."

Again writing to my parents under date of May 14th and 15th, I say:

"The news is more encouraging now than it has been of late. I see by a late issue of a Cincinnati paper that General [Ambrose] Burnside has sentenced Vallaningham for two years on the Tortugas. Well, if this be true, it is good news to us soldiers in the field, for that man is doing us more harm in our rear than the Rebel army is doing us in front.

Clement Laird Vallandigham (1820–1871) was an Ohio politician and a leader of the Copperheads, Northern Democrats who were anti-war.—Ed. 2017

"General Burnside is the right man in the right place exactly in the right time. I learn that he has over one hundred thousand men under his command in the State of Kentucky, and I believe he is just the man to handle them.

"I must tell you that I am much pleased with our field and-staff officers. Colonel Strickland is a fine officer; he is kind to his men, and although he is a small man, he is full of grit, and if I don't miss my guess, if he gets the chance, will come home with the stars on his shoulders. Lieutenant Colonel Cook was a good officer, but he has left us. George R. Elsner is our Lieutenant Colonel now, and he is a fine looking officer; kind to the men; will make his mark if he remains in the service, but is useless for me to mention the officers personally; take them as a whole, the officers of the regiment with but few exceptions are first-class, and will compare very favorable with any other regimental officers in the service.

"Lieutenant Moore took a non-commissioned officer and three privates and going out into the country, arrested and brought into camp three prisoners and five or six muskets. This morning, it is said that one of the prisoners shot at some of our men the other day. I do not know what disposition will be made of them, but suppose if they are found guilty, they will be sent to prison.

"Do not worry about me. I am in the best of health and spirits.

"I am going to try and get a pass or furlough in a few days, and take a run home, and see you all, but as I have said before, do not look for me until you see me coming. In the meantime, trust in God, and hope for the best."

May 25th:

"Feel very much disappointed. My company officers made me out a furlough, and I went to Colonel Strickland to get his signature to it and he refused to sign it at present, giving as his reason that there were too many of the boys away at this time. Later on he said, when some of them had returned, my furlough should be granted, so I will try to be patient.

"This is a beautiful day; the sun is shining in all her splendor, making the shade of the woods delightful and cool. The early flowers are bursting into bloom, and the birds, as they dart among the leafy branches of the trees, are singing their sweetest songs.

"On such a day as this, if it was not for cruel war and other wickedness that is being carried on in the world, the whole human family could be happy. Our hearts would be filled with peace and joy, and the sunshine would be brighter, the grass would be greener, the shade of the trees would be cooler, the songs of the birds would be sweeter, and the perfume of the flowers more fragrant.

"Oh, when will the day come when men will cease their wickedness; when will they cease warring with each other, and learn to live in peace."

June 14th:

"Well, I suppose you have been looking for me home the last few days pretty strongly, but I must tell you there has been too much excitement here for a few days to think of leaving here on a furlough.

"There had been a band of the enemy's hovering around here for a few days, and yesterday morning, as the freight train arrived at Elizabethtown, the band made a dash into town, and captured ten carloads of horses and broke open a safe that contained quite a large sum of money. While they were busy unloading their captured property, someone reported to them that the whole Fiftieth Ohio Regiment was coming and they pulled up stakes and left. Two or three companies of the regiment did go up, but, of course, the Rebels were up and gone by the time they got there. No use of infantry trying to catch cavalry."

June 24th:

"Quiet once more reigns in the camp on Muldraugh's Hill, and things move along as they did before without a ripple to disturb the smooth surface.

"Captain Hendricks has resigned and gone home, McClure will now come in as Captain, and Pine as First Lieutenant, and Vandurson as Second Lieutenant. I have given up the furlough business for the present time.

"A rumor in camp that John Morgan has invaded Kentucky once more."

One of the most enjoyable features of a soldier's life is receiving letters from the loved ones at home, and from friends and sweethearts. To the married men, it was indeed a feast of good things to get a letter from their wives, telling all the news of home; how things were prospering in their absence; how fast little Willie was growing; and how many teeth the baby had, and how the poor lonely wife breathed a prayer of hope that the cruel war would soon close; that they might welcome the husband and father home once more to their arms. Ah, yes! how eagerly those men would grasp their letters and steal away from the noisy crowd, that they might read them in secret, for those letters were sacred to them alone. They wished to be alone with God, when they read them, for they were the golden links that bound them to the loving ones at home. Then there were the letters from parents, brothers and sisters; how we did enjoy reading them; how they did brighten our lives, driving away the gloomy shadows, and letting in the bright sunshine, and last though not least, were the letters we youngsters received from the girls we left behind us.

As someone has truthfully said, "They warmed our hearts like sunshine and cheered our souls like old wine, give us hope for the future and blotted out the past"; what encouragements and good cheer they gave us; how we did prize those sweet messages; how we did bless the man that first invented paper, ink and pens. Yes, their letters to us were what the green oasis is to the weary traveler in the desert. They were refreshing and restful. God pity the soldier that has no kind friends to write to him; his lot is a hard one.

NEWS OF MORGAN'S CAPTURE

The rumor in regard to John Morgan entering Kentucky again proved true, as it was at this time that he started on his famous raid through Kentucky, Indiana and Ohio.

He came in over the Columbia and Lebanon turnpike, the same route that we took our memorial ride after him on New Year's Day. He attacked a small force of our men on the hill south of Green River bridge, and was handsomely repulsed; leaving them, he made his way to Lebanon, where he attacked another small force of our men, and defeated them taking them prisoners, and if I remember rightfully, his brother was killed in this engagement.

He marched his prisoners as far as Springfield, a short distance from Lebanon, and there he paroled them, and proceeded on his way. His movements from this on are familiar to all who have read the history of this daring raider, and his bold troops as he had burnt the trestle here on one of his former raids. We all supposed he would try the same feat again, and this caused us to be very watchful while he was anywhere near our vicinity. We were called out every morning at 2 o'clock, and would remain in our forts and breastworks until after daylight, and we kept this up, I think, for nearly a week.

One morning during the time, probably the last morning, we were called out. We were lounging about in the fort and rifle pits, and it was just beginning to get daylight when there were three reports like the discharge of cannon following each other in rapid succession at the lower trestle, where the first battalion was encamped; in an instant every man was on his feet, and in his rightful place in the works. My gun squad rushed to their places, and we run the gun up, and had her muzzle sticking out the port hole ready for business. At first we thought sure that Morgan had opened the ball at the lower camp, and we stood and listened and watched till long after daylight, but all was quiet after those three discharges. We found out at last that the boys were blasting some rocks out of the way down there, and had let them off at that hour in the morning to have a joke on us of the second battalion. Well, they had their joke all right, for it raised quite a little breeze among us for a short time.

Some of the boys told the following little joke on a certain captain in our battalion. That morning when the three blasts went off, this captain wished to deploy his men as skirmishers along the rifle pits, but laboring under a little bit of excitement, he forgot his tactics, so he gave the following command: "Company! as skirmishers, along the breastworks, fly out," but the boys did not move, seeing which, the captain continued: "Fly out, boys, fly out, been in the service for nearly a year and don't know how to fly out yet." Whether the poor captain really used such language or not, I am not prepared to say, but I know the boys run the joke on him pretty strong, and did not permit him to forget it for many a long day.

There had been a bunch of hogs running about our camp for some time. Lieutenant Colonel Elsner had put up notices, warning the owners if they did not take their hogs away before a certain date, he would not be responsible-for them. The date of the warning had run out, and the hogs were still running about camp in good condition, and Colonel Elsner before dismissing us that morning, gave each company permission to slaughter one of those fat hogs, so if the first battalion did have the joke on us in regards to the rock blasting, we were one ahead of them on the fresh pork business. Thus John Morgan passed us by, and went on his way, but I have no doubt his scouts viewed our camps and fortifications from a distance, and perhaps the General took a peep at them himself. I have sometimes thought that perhaps he would have given us a call if his pursuers had not crowded him so close, but as it was, he had to keep moving for fear the boys in blue would close in on him. Then again I have thought it was not his intention to do much fighting on this raid. Self-interest was the moving cause of his actions. His chief object was plunder, to astonish the natives, and build up for himself a grand reputation as a daring and fearless raider, in all of which, he was in a manner successful, though in the final wind-up he landed in-prison.

But now he had passed beyond our jurisdiction, our camps on Muldraugh's Hill settled down once more to our regular routine duty. The boys once more made their morning calls on Mother Casey under the hill to get their accustomed glass of chain lightning, and everything and everybody moved along in the same old beaten track as before, only we scanned the papers eagerly from day to day to see where the bold riders were, and what they were doing, and must say we were somewhat surprised when we learned they had crossed the Ohio River, and were raiding through the State of Indiana. Then again came the news they had entered our own beautiful State of Ohio, and were forging ahead almost at the gates of the Queen City, and we knew not but what the next news that would be flashed over the wires would be that they had captured the city, and that General Morgan had pitched his headquarters' tent on Fountain Square. But instead in a few days, we received the joyful news that the Yankee troops had finally cornered the wily rebel chief, and compelled him to surrender and that our General Burnside had assigned Morgan and some of his officers, quarters in the Ohio Penitentiary, where they could rest for a few days in security.

The following appears in a letter to my father, dated July 28th:

"The news of Morgan's capture was received here yesterday with great rejoicing. Yes, we all feel happy over it, for we have all lost more sleep watching for Morgan since we entered the service than from any other cause. Guess General Burnside will see to it that he won't disturb our rest for a while at least, but he certainly did give our men a race for their money. One big advantage he had being in the lead he got all the fresh horses he wanted, while our forces were obliged to use their jaded animals, almost the entire trip.

Well, it has given the Indiana and Ohio people a little taste of war, and they will have something to think of and talk over for some time to come.

"There is a rumor in camp today that we are ordered to Mobile, but I judge it came in over the grapevine *Telaliegraph*" [tell-a-lie-gram] line, and like a great many other rumors we have had, will prove to be a joke. There are some of the boys who take delight in starting these groundless rumors, as there is a class that is always ready to believe any old tale that is told them, and this is great sport for those who operate the grapevine line."

We found our tents pretty hot in the daytime, toward the last of July and the first of August, so that when we had no duty to perform, we sought the pleasant shade of the trees near camp, and many a letter was written under their cool and sheltering boughs.

All was quiet in our camp on Muldraugh's Hill at this time, except a false alarm now and then when some nervous picket on the outpost would fire on some innocent cow or hog that he would, in his over-wrought imagination, take to be the foe trying to steal a march on him. A shot or two by the pickets would alarm the camp and cause us all to be called out under arms, and remain there until the officers of the day would visit the outpost where the firing had taken place, and learn what the trouble was. We had a number of such alarms while guarding those trestles.

In one instance, I remember, the picket fired on and killed an old sow that belonged to Mother Casey, the chain lightning-dealer. I do not remember how the matter was settled, but this fatal shot made quite a number of orphans, as the old sow had a nice litter of young pigs at the time.

Some of the boys had a trick of getting down by the railroad with a stick and, as the passenger trains would be passing, knock the passengers' hats off, as they would lean out the windows to get a peep at our camp. Several lost their fine hats in this way before the commanding officers found it out and put a stop to the boys' fun.

I don't want the reader to get the impression that the Fiftieth Ohio boys were any more vicious than the boys in other regiments, but will say that for downright, Simon-pure devilishness, the boys of the Fiftieth would keep their end of the log up without overtaxing their muscles a particle. Some of them were just simply bubbling over with mischief at all hours.

A few of the boys would scrap among themselves at times, but the main reason of this, I think I can safely say, was because they got too much of Mother Casey's chain lightning [whiskey] aboard. Two of Company "K's" boys had a small scrap at the supper table one evening and one of them had a hole cut in his head with a rock, and bled like a stuck hog. We none of us sympathized with him a great deal, for he was quite a quarrelsome chap when drinking, and, this day, he had been at Mother Casey's or somewhere else, and was loaded to the guards with chain lightning or "Kill me quick," and that got him into trouble. When he was sober, there was no trouble to get along with him and if there was a hog or sheep anywhere near camp, you could bet your bottom dollar he would have one for his mess, but this stone business settled him down. I do not remember that the boys had any more trouble with him afterwards.

I will just say here, as I will bring him to the front three or four times before I close this story, that his name was Andrew Jackson Culp.

Many of the boys, while at Muldraugh's Hill, received boxes of eatables and other useful articles from home. The writer was one among the happy number. I say happy because they came to us as pleasant reminders that we were not forgotten by the loved ones at home. Ah! how we did enjoy those good things that mothers' and sisters' dear hands had prepared for us. How vividly did it bring to our minds the picture of that dear old home, as we once more tasted of the pickles, preserves and sweetmeats, that our kindly old mothers had taken such care to prepare. In our minds' eye, we could see father, mother, sisters and brothers as they placed those things lovingly in the box; all were interested, all had something to send the absent one.

Yes, we can even imagine we can see the tears as they silently steal down the furrowed cheeks and drop one by one as sweet messages of love to the soldier boy, as he stands on the lonely picket, with the twinkling stars above him, or lays dreaming in his tent in the quiet hours of night, but could they have looked on our happy, smiling faces as we opened and looked on these precious gifts, they would have been well paid for their loving care and thoughtfulness, for our hearts were filled to overflowing with love, gratitude and joy to know that the dear ones at home still thought of the absent ones, and we fully appreciated their thoughtful kindness in sending us these rich gifts as loving tokens of their remembrance.

The following is an extract from a letter I sent home after receiving my box:

"Fort Sands, Big Run Trestle, L. & N. R. R.,

August 16, 1863.

"Dear Parents, Brothers and Sisters:—I take the opportunity today of answering your very welcome letter I received a few days ago. It was pleasant news to hear you were all in good health. Please accept my thanks for your very nice letter. The box you sent me reached me with the contents all in a good state of preservation. You may rest assured that I thoroughly enjoyed the many good things that you sent me. The sight of them and the taste of them brought thoughts to my mind of the dear old home, and for a moment I could almost imagine that I was in your midst. What made it doubly dear to me, it came as a birthday gift. I was 20 years of age the 8th of August. I consider myself almost a man now. I guess I ought to be, as I weigh 180 pounds, and am in perfect health. I am the heaviest man in Company "K."

"Jerry Ammerman's father was here to see him a few days ago. He said he thought the boys looked fine. Jerry is the bass drummer in our band and is a good boy.

"The weather here has been extremely warm for some time, find it pretty hot in our tents in the day time, but pleasant at night.

"I must not close this letter without telling you that I appreciated the things you sent me very much, and I thank you all from the depths of my heart for your kind remembrance of the absent one. May pleasant memories of the pleasure and enjoyment they afforded me linger lovingly in my heart while life shall last. May God bless you all is the fervent wish and prayer of your affectionate son and brother."

This will show the reader how we boys in blue enjoyed the good things sent us from our far-away homes, and do not think for a moment we were selfish with them. No, but we shared them with those who were less fortunate than ourselves, and by so doing, we brought a little of our bright and happy sunshine into their dark lives that perhaps would have been sad and dreary without it, and let us hope it made them better men and better soldiers.

"Fort Sands, Ky., September 8, 1863.

"We are having very easy times here at present. We have finished fortifying, so all we do is drill about four hours a day, and once a week stand our turn of guard. The balance of the time each one is trying to see how much pleasure and enjoyment he can crowd into the few days that we remain here, for there are rumors in the air that our days here are nearly numbered, and none of us know what our destiny will be when we leave this place, but whatever comes to our lot, we will try to meet it as we have in the past, with that earnest zeal and courage that should animate every true soldier of the Union to keep his name untarnished and permit that dear old flag that we all love to be trailed in the dust.

"Quite a number of women and young girls from out in the country visit our camps daily to sell us boys cakes, pies and fruit. We youngsters have our own fun with them. I wish you could see and taste some of the so-called sweet potato pies that are brought in here to sell. We make all kinds of sport of them, and tell the women and girls that they made a mistake and put the shortening in the long way. I did buy some custard pies up in Elizabethtown the other day that were all right; they tasted like the ones mother used to make, and I enjoyed them fine. But those we buy here are simply boiled sweet potatoes wrapped up in a little dough, mixed up with water, and placed in an oven or out in the hot sun and dried. You can imagine how they taste, but as the jackass said when he ate the thistles: 'They do to fill up on.'

"Some of the boys did have a habit awhile back of slipping out into the country after roll call at night to court the girls, but the Colonel got onto their game and sent out and had them arrested and put them on double duty and had them digging up stumps at his headquarters. That has put a damper on the courting biz.

"Lieutenant Pine is at Louisville on Court Martial duty, and Captain McClure is also on detached service somewhere in Kentucky. Company "K" is now under command of Lieutenant John McCloe, of Company "I"; he is a Cincinnatian; a splendid little officer and one that understands his business. There has been no stirring news from the different armies for some time. Rosy [William Rosecrans] and Burnside are watching Bragg. [Frederick] Steele is watching [Confederate General Sterling] Price; Mead[e] is watching Lee, and [artillery expert General Quincy Adams] Gilmore is throwing Greek fire into Charleston, so we may reasonably expect a rumpus to be kicked up among some of them before long, as a storm is almost certain to follow a calm."

The letter immediately above is obviously written after the twin victories of Gettysburg (July 3) and Vicksburg (July 4). Union General George Gordon Meade had been given command of the Army of the Potomac just three days before Gettysburg. Ulysses S. Grant had had

Vicksburg under siege for months. The capture of the latter cut the Confederacy in half and gave the Union control of the Mississippi River.— Ed. 2017

Well, the rumors that had been flying through our camps for several days that we were going to move was on the 16th day of September fully confirmed, as on that day we received orders to get ready to march, but did not break camp until the 18th, when we marched as far as Elizabethtown and went into camp. It was with many regrets that we took leave of the camps, where we had passed so many happy days, but we were soldiers serving Uncle Sam and must go where those in command thought we could render the best service; so we sadly turned our backs on the old camp grounds, and marched away, bidding each familiar object an affectionate farewell. Yes, the time had finally arrived when we must say good bye to Muldraugh's Hill and all her pleasant associations; no more should we, as lonely sentinels stand on picket on her borders, with no sound to disturb the solitude through the long dreary night hours but the never-ceasing voices of the whippoorwills; no more shall the hoot of the owl from his perch in the old dead oak startle us from our pleasant dreams in the quiet hour of midnight; farewell all you fair ones, whose bright and happy faces have so often brought joy and gladness into our hearts; we must leave you, but rest assured wherever we go, we shall never forget the pleasant hours we have passed together, and we trust your good wishes shall follow us; and last, though not least, those of us who have patronized Mother Casey's under the hill, and have so often been regaled by the contents of her old brown jug, have said good bye to her, as we sipped our farewell drink, while the tears coursed slowly down our cheeks (was it the strength of the liquor, or the thoughts of parting caused them, who shall say?)

Thus we have said our last good byes. Strangers shall now take up the work where we leave it. Mother Casey shall continue to retail chain lightning from the same old brown jug, but it will not be our shin plasters that will help to swell her bank account.

The bright smiles of the fair ones shall still bring joy and gladness into the hearts of the boys in blue, but not for us who shall be far away. The whippoorwills shall still continue their all-night concerts, but other ears than ours shall listen to their music; and the solemn old owl, from his station in the oak, shall look down on the strangers and blinking his eyes shall croak: "Who, who are you?"

GLASGOW TO NASHVILLE TO GLASGOW

When we arrived at Elizabethtown, we proudly unfurled Old Glory to the breeze and marched through the town, led by our band, playing national airs, and went into camp just outside the town limits, it was said at the time to await transportation on the cars; this was on Friday afternoon. Saturday, the paymaster arrived and paid us off, but as he deducted the last year's clothing account, there were not many of the boys that received much cash, as we had nearly all overdrawn our amount.

I was put on some kind of guard duty on Saturday; I do not remember now what it was for, but in the dusk of the evening as I was returning to camp through town, in crossing a little bridge, I stumbled over some obstacle and stooping down and picking it up, I found it to be a pair of holster pistols that belonged to Colonel Strickland, or, at least, were claimed by him the next morning, and I turned them over to him, and he never so much as said: "Thank you," for them.

On Saturday, we were told to be ready to march Sunday morning at 7 o'clock, so I suppose the transportation rumor was one of those grapevine *"Telaliegrams"*

"Glasgow, Ky., September 24, 1863.

"We left Elizabethtown Sunday morning at 7 o'clock, marching till noon, when we halted for dinner at Camp Nervine at the Red Hills on Nolin Creek. After resting an hour, we resumed our march until night, when we went into camp on Williams' branch, Larue County; distance from Elizabethtown, twenty miles. Next morning, again took up the line of march and at noon crossed Bacon Creek and halted for dinner. After a good rest, we again forged ahead and, at night, reached Mumfordsville on the Green River. We camped below the town in an orchard, and Colonel Strickland treated us to all the beer we wanted to drink. There are several forts around the town and I was told there had been several skirmishes taken place here. It is not much of a town.

"On the morning of the 22nd, we again resumed our march. We were halted to rest a short distance from Mumfordsville, in front of what appeared the residence of a well-to-do farmer. Colonel Strickland and his staff officers seated themselves on the porch, and were conversing very pleasantly with the farmer, when a servant appeared and announced that some of the soldiers had paid a visit to the meat house, and that there was a ham missing. Colonel Strickland at once became very indignant, and had the regiment called up into line and searched, but no ham was found. So we resumed our march, the boys singing a song, only a few words of which I now recall, and they were: 'Johnnie stole the ham, way down in *Alabam*.'

"At noon we reached Cave City and halted for dinner, and I think it quite likely the Colonel had fried ham for his dinner. Cave City is not far from the famous Mammoth Cave that we had read and heard so much about. I was told there are quite a number of caves hereabout, and it is for that reason the town has been named Cave City.

"After dinner, we once more took up the line of march, and camped for the night on the banks of Beaver Creek, two miles from Glasgow, and yesterday, the 23rd, we came on into town. There are several regiments here at present, but we are not likely to remain here very long, for the air is full of flying rumors. Will try and keep you posted at home by letter wherever we go.

"We had a very nice march. The country was mostly level that we passed through. We had our knapsacks hauled, and that was quite a relief to us. The distance from here to Elizabethtown, I am told, is sixty-five miles.

"You shall hear from me again in a few days."

"Nashville, Tennessee, September 27, 1863.

"The very night after writing you all that letter from Glasgow, we received marching orders, and next morning at daylight we were on the move, and at noon we reached Cave City; distance from Glasgow, twelve miles. We halted and remained there until late in the evening. We were then put aboard the cars, and early yesterday morning, we arrived in Nashville. They have a fine State House here, and what little I have seen of the country around here I am delighted with it. There are several large forts built here; some of them bombproof, but while the country pleases me, there is an element among the inhabitants here at this time that is inclined to be pretty tough, but, as you well know, I never mingle with that class if I can avoid it, but it is almost impossible for a soldier to avoid it always. There is a strong talk in camp that a part of our regiment will be sent back to help guard the railroad between here and Elizabethtown."

"Nashville, Tennessee, October 8, 1863.

"There are but five companies of our regiment here at the present time. Three companies are at Gallatin and the other two are at different places guarding the railroad. There are not many troops here at present, and guard duty is pretty heavy. We have, a line to picket around Nashville said to be twenty miles in length. Our five companies guard five miles of the line; that brings us on duty every third day. I see plenty of rebels here, but they are tame. There is a jail full of them near our camp.

"By the way, it is just a year ago today since we received our first introduction to the Rebs at Perryville, Ky. They did not impress me at that time as being very polite.

"I may not be here when you hear from me again, for as usual the camp is full of rumors."

We did not remain in Nashville many days, and I do not know as any of the boys regretted leaving there, for the guard duty was rather hard on us. Then again it was hardly safe for a man in Nashville at this time to appear on the streets after night, especially if he had any valuables on his person, for the toughs would hold him up and rob him, and, to tell the truth, he was fortunate if he got away with his life. This mugging or robbery came very near causing trouble between the Fiftieth Ohio and another regiment near us one night, but fortunately it was settled without bloodshed, but for a time the outlook was bright for a drawn battle between the two regiments. I believe the trouble arose over a man being knocked down and robbed between the two camps.

I cannot give the date we left Nashville, as I have no letters or memorandum to refer to that throws any light on it. I only can say we left there sometime towards the end of October.

"Fort Boil, No. 1, Glasgow, Ky., Oct. 30, 1863.

"Well, we are back at Glasgow again. I have just come in off of picket and as it rained all night I had a wet time of it, but that's nothing when a fellow gets used to it.

I would rather be a soldier fighting for the honor of the old flag, as every American boy ought to, than to be a cowardly butternut and set around the fire and toast my shins those stormy nights. It seems to me if they had the courage of their conviction, it would look more honorable on their part, but, no, they stay at home and shake their fists in their pockets and backbite us fellows who are out here trying to protect their homes. Shame on them!

"We have here with us the Thirty-seventh Kentucky mounted infantry and the Sixth Michigan battery. Part of the Thirty-seventh Kentucky was captured here the last of September, but they are all paroled and here with us again. There are only five companies of the Fiftieth Ohio here at the present; three companies are at Gallatin, between here and Nashville, and one on Nolin Creek, near Elizabethtown. There are plenty of Rebels in this part of the country, and they may make a break on us some of these mornings. Well, if they do, we will give them the best we got in the shop; that's all we can do.

"I am in very good health except for a bad cold that has bothered me for a few days, but it has about passed off now, unless I take a fresh one by getting so wet last night."

Glasgow, Barren County, Ky., November 17, 1863.

"You ask me how I am enjoying myself. In answer I will say that I am enjoying myself as well as a soldier can expect. I have plenty to eat and plenty to wear; good quarters to stay in and plenty of good friends; of course, my surroundings are not quite as pleasant as they would be at home; that could not be expected under the circumstances, but I just say that I have no complaint to bring against anyone in the regiment. That you may judge of the friendly feeling toward me, let me inform you that I have not had a word of dispute with any officer or private in my mess, company or regiment since I enlisted. I would not say that I am clear of faults, not by any means, but I try to treat everyone with courtesy, and obey my officers promptly; in short, I practice the Golden Rule, and. by so doing, I have won the confidence and respect of my officers and comrades.

"We have built very neat quarters here. We first put up the frames and weather-boarded them, and for a roof, we use our shelter tents; that makes a very comfortable house; there are six men in my tent, and we have a small sheet iron stove, and when we all get in there and have a good fire we are as cozy as you please.

"I wish we could stay here for the winter, but I think that is rather doubtful from the present outlook, as matters appear to be very Unsettled here at present; the grapevine *"Telaliegraph"* line is kept hot these days with all sorts of rumors. There was a rumor the other day that there was a band of rebels near town; a detail of scouts went out but returned without seeing any Rebs.

"About 12 o'clock yesterday a report came in that the Rebs had captured two of our battery wagons that were out after forage, but like the other rumors, it proved to be a fake. So it goes. 'Rebels, Rebels, Rebels,' is the cry, but so far, they have failed to materialize. I believe I came as near seeing Rebs last Sunday night as some of the others have. I had three men with me on picket on the Bowling Green road. About 10 o'clock in the evening four horsemen approached the outpost. He called out: 'Halt' to them, and they wheeled their horses, and rode away on the jump. The sentry should have fired on them, but failed to do so. There was a lane leading off the main road past an old slaughter house, two or three hundred yards in the rear of the reserve post, and we kept hearing horses passing through the lane, so I posted a man about half way from the reserve to the lane, with orders to find out if possible what they were up to. Pretty soon I heard the tramp of a horse in the lane once more, and the voice of my sentry sung out, 'Halt, halt, halt, who goes there,' and then that old musket of his spoke out loud and clear, and the fire spouted front the muzzle; it seemed to me a hundred feet, and maybe that horse did not get up and go. The guard reported that there was a man on the horse, but he must have shot too high, as I don't think he touched horse or man. However, we were not disturbed after that. All remained quiet, but before that, there were all kinds of noises around us. Now, I think, they were Rebels trying to sneak up and capture us, but finding us wide awake they gave it up as a bad job. When daylight came I went over into the lane and, although the ground was frozen, I could see the marks that horse made in his efforts to get away when that old musket cracked. You may be sure there was no sleeping done by any of us that night at our post."

"While we were at Glasgow we received orders that when we turned out to roll call in the mornings we should come out under arms. Of course, that included the commissioned officers, as well as the privates. All went well for a while, although some of the chronic grumblers found fault with the order and thought it was unnecessary.

"One morning the commanding officer of Company "K" came out without his sword. One of our boys (a young German), took notice of it immediately and began to curse and swear that it was as much the duty of the officer to turn out with his sword on as it was for us to turn out with our guns, and as he was not particular to speak in a low tone the officer heard him, and after they had exchanged a few angry words with each other the officer handed the writer a rope and ordered him to take the comrade up to the flag staff and tie him up. In the meantime, a report had been taken to Colonel Strickland's headquarters by one of the comrade's friends, and just as the writer had completed tying the comrade. Adjutant Crowley appeared on the scene with an open knife and cut the comrade loose and told him to go to his quarters. I reported to my commanding officer what had taken place and he started out for Strickland's headquarters in a hurry, but he must have received a cool reception as that closed the incident."

I will add here that several years after the war, this same comrade came to visit me in Kentucky, and I was greatly surprised to see what a mighty change had taken place in him. He could talk on any subject you might bring up fluently and interestingly.

He had become a strict member of the German Methodist Church, and I believe he sometimes does a little preaching for them. He told me that he gave his wife the credit of bringing about the great reformation in him.

"Glasgow, December 6, 1863.

"I am still in good health and spirits. Guard duty is rather heavy on us at the present time, as the Thirty-seventh Kentucky Regiment are most all engaged in scouting. They are mounted infantry. Hence they use them the same as cavalry. They bring in prisoners every day. The Rebel General Hamilton is hovering around here all the time, and now we hear that John Morgan has escaped and that he passed within eight miles of here yesterday, and that Hamilton was to meet him with four or five hundred men and escort him to Tennessee.

"All is very quiet in camp today as it is Sunday. Labor and drill are put aside. The sky is cloudless and the sun shines very pleasant and warm for December.

"I was on picket the entire night, and a well-dressed gentleman came up to my outpost and wanted to pass into Glasgow. Said he was a doctor and lived in town. Now, I had orders to let no one in or out without a pass, but I generally use my own judgment in such matters, and told such a straight story that I passed him on into town. I have studied about it since. Perhaps it was John Morgan. He was a dark-complected, good-looking man; well-dressed and appeared to be much of a gentleman. I have never heard anything of him since, but if I had it to do over again he would remain at my post until someone higher in the ranks than I would pass him along.

"We have the Sixth Michigan Battery with us here. They are a fine body of men, and our boys and the battery boys get along very nicely together. I love to watch them drill. Sometimes they go out in the field and drill the same as infantry, and when they move off in two ranks they keep perfect step, and it interests me very much as I take great delight in watching well-drilled troops go through the different military movements. There is only about half of the Fiftieth here. I do not know positive where the others are, but have heard they were at Louisville."

Nothing worthy of note took place while we were at Glasgow. Colonel Strickland had us roused out two or three times at night to test the Thirty-seventh Kentucky and the Fiftieth Ohio to see how quickly he could get us all in line, and into the fort in case we were attacked. Company drill, battalion drill and picketing the different roads was the routine for the Fiftieth boys, while a portion of the Thirty-seventh Kentucky boys were continually on the scout. I would have enjoyed a trip to Mammoth Cave while here, but was not permitted that pleasure. I was told it was only nine miles from Glasgow.

So the uneventful days passed by until the 14th of December rolled round, when we again received marching orders.

OVER THE CUMBERLAND MOUNTAINS

Marching orders. What! leave our pleasant quarters where we had such high hopes we would be permitted to pass the winter? "Yes," says the orderly sergeant. "Company 'K' be ready to move in the morning at 7 o'clock." So on the morning of the 15th of December we shouldered our knapsacks and swung out into the road that led to Columbia, Ky., and soon the pretty little town of Glasgow was left in our rear. We were sorry, of course, to leave our cozy quarters, for we had become quite attached to them, but when we saw our dear old flag once more unfurled to the breeze and saw the December sun kissing her billowy folds, while the band played our old favorite air of "Rally round the flag, boys," we moved off with a firm step determined to cheerfully go where ever duty called us.

Our attention was called to various interesting scenes along the line of march, and soon our comfortable camp that we had left at Glasgow was forgotten.

At intervals, we would pass some rich old Kentucky Colonel's residence and there would be a crowd of wooly heads at the side of the road to see us pass; they would be all ages from the little one in arms to the old, white-haired mamma, or the old, gray-haired patriarch. They would roll up the whites of their eyes and show their ivorys, as the boys would call to them to take off their hats. Hats, did I say? Well, they may have once borne that name, but now it would puzzle one to find a name that would fit them. Some were crownless; some were rimless; some had been made of wool, and others of straw, but they all had that woe-begone appearance, as though they had passed through a Kansas cyclone, or rather a Kansas cyclone had passed through them, but nevertheless, these poor darkies would jerk them off. and stand with their wooly heads uncovered, while the boys in blue were marching by. Very few white folks were to be seen. While a goodly number of them had joined the South, another goodly number of them had joined the North, and when they met on the field of battle, it was Greek meeting Greek. Kentuckians made good soldiers and they were fighters as both the North and South can bear witness.

Nothing of interest happened to us on this march. That is, nothing worthy of making a note of.

I make a few extracts here from a letter I wrote after reaching Columbia.

"Columbia, Ky., December 22, 1863.

"I suppose you will be somewhat surprised to hear that we are at Columbia again, but nevertheless it is true.

"We left Glasgow on the morning of the 15th, and after a rather hard march, we arrived here on the morning of the 17th. The Fiftieth is all together once more. Four companies that had been guarding rebel prisoners to Rock Island, Ill., joined us today. The Third Kentucky Battery and a battalion of the Thirteenth Kentucky Cavalry are here also. Kittle did we think when we left this place one year ago today that we would be back here in one year, but such is the fact.

"We are camped one mile west of the town; twenty-four men of Company "K" are down in the town as provost guards. I hear we will leave here in a few days again and march to Somerset, Ky. Well, there is only two more days till Christmas. I would love to be home and eat dinner with you all that day, but, of course, that is not possible. But I shall think of you all and whisper: 'Do they miss me at home, do they miss me?'

"I will write again in a few days and let you know where I am. I wish you all a Happy Christmas and a Merry New Year."

The next evening after our arrival at Columbia, Sergeant Sam Lousy proposed to me that we would go out to some of the farmers, and get supper. Of course, I did not refuse. I was not built that way. After going perhaps a mile from camp, we called at a house and were met by two ladies, a mother and daughter. The sergeant politely asked them if they could prepare supper for us; they answered him in the affirmative, and we were invited into the house and given seats by the fire, and the ladies went to work to prepare the meal. The young lady, it appeared, was pretty well educated, and had taught school some little. It did not take us long to learn from their talk (and by the way, they were both well blessed with the gift of gab), that their sympathy were all on the side of those that wore the gray, and that they had no particular use for those that were clothed with the regulation blue; they called down anything but blessings on the heads of those Yankee vandals that had robbed them of their sheep, hogs and chickens. We agreed with them, and said such doings were all wrong, and that the scamps ought to be punished for treating the citizens that way.

Seeing that we sided with them, they were encouraged to come down still heavier on those awful "Yanks," and Lousy and I pitied the poor fellows wherever they were that evening, for we felt sure their ears were burning like fire. We were innocent as babes, of course. At last, the ladies announced that our supper was ready; they took us out into a newly built log kitchen, that had never been chinked yet, and there were cracks between the logs that a large Newfoundland dog could have jumped through and never touched a hair. In this well ventilated dining room, we sat down to a fairly good supper, but Greenland's Icy Mountains! how cold it was in that room. It would have been warmer outdoors entirely; there was a cold wind blowing, and the way it did whistle through those cracks was something fierce; the cold shivers played hide and seek up and down our spinal columns and our teeth would have rattled together had we not kept them otherwise employed, and, to tell the truth, we were glad when the meal was ended. Lousy asked the lady what the charges were, and was told that it was fifty cents for the two; he presented a five dollar bill, railroad money, but the lady said she could not change it. "Well," says Lousy, "What are we to do, that is all we have," but on second thought, says he, "If you will send your colored boy to camp with us, we will get the bill changed and send your fifty cents back by the boy."

But this she refused to do as Lousy well knew she would, for I suppose she surmised if she sent the boy to our camp, that would be the last she would see of him and very likely it would have been, but Lousy still had another proposition up his sleeve, which he now brought forth: "Lady," he says with one of his blandest smiles, "You prepare breakfast for us in the morning and we will be here about sunrise and then we will have the change, and pay for the four meals" The madam said that would be satisfactory, 'and we bid them good evening and departed. The ladies may be waiting breakfast for

Lousy and me yet for aught I know, as we never went back to see. It was one of Sergeant Lousy's Yankee tricks from start to finish for the five dollar bill was no good.

We might have paid them if they had not been so bitter against the Yankees, and then to cap the climax, they tried to freeze us to death, while we were eating, so we called it a square deal. It is safe to say that was not the first or the last meal Sergeant Lousy got on the strength of that five dollar bill.

The favorite drink around Columbia at this time was the famous Kentucky "Apple Jack."

We remained here until Christmas morning, when we once more broke camp and started towards Somerset, which is near Burnside point on the Cumberland River.

"Camp near Somerset, Ky., December 30, 1863.

"Well, what I told you all in my letter from Columbia proved true. We left Columbia on Christmas morning and it was said we marched about 24 miles. We passed through a wild country that day; we never saw more than three or four houses on the way. It was rather a dull Christmas for us youngsters. We camped at night in a piece of woods. On the morning of the 26th we resumed our march. Did not make quite as many miles as we did on Christmas. Camped at night in some tobacco sheds and barns, the owners kindly granting us that privilege. Resuming our march on the 27th, we had to wade Fishing Creek, the water coming up nearly to our armpits, while the clouds above us were sending down on our heads a regular downpour, but after crossing, we went into the salt works and camped for the night. Building large fires, we soon got our clothing dry. The owner of the works being a rebel, we confiscated all his hogs and also a large barrel of sauerkraut. On the 28th, we reached here and are camped about half a mile west of the town.

This was a pretty hard march on us, because it rained so much while w-e were on the road. One evening we camped in an open field while on the march from Glasgow to Columbia, and there came up a heavy thunder shower. A comrade and I saw it coming, and we grabbed up our harness and went to a nearby barn, and made our bed in an ox stall, and, oh! what a nice sleep we had. We came into camp the next morning as dry as you please, while the boys in camp looked like drowned rats.

On the way here, we passed the battlefield of Mill Springs, where [Confederate General Felix] Zollycoffer [sic] was killed. I saw the graves of eighteen soldiers that were killed there. Six of the Ninth Ohio and twelve of the Second Minnesota. The graves were fixed up very nicely.

"We had inspection today and Colonel Strickland rode out in front of us and made us a short speech. Among other things he told us, we had been ordered to Knoxville, Tennessee, so, therefore, he said we had ten days' march before us, and over the Cumberland Mountains at that, so likely the next time you hear from me I will be in Knoxville.

"Well, if I keep my health as good as it is now, I think I will get through all right. The old year is drawing to a close. Soon the last page in the history of 1863 will be written, and a new history will be commenced on a clean and spotless page, dated at the top, January 1, 1864. How long will it be before its beautiful clean pages will be blotted with accounts of wicked crimes and misery. It may be the historian will have, to record on that first bright new page, the history of a bloody battle, who can tell? We cannot read the future, but judging the future by the past, we can safely say that the history of 1864 will not have many pages but what will be darkly stained by the record of cruel and bloody war, and will the close of 1864 see the close of the war? Alas! who can tell? But-let us hope it may. I will write you again as soon as I can."

This march from Columbia to Somerset was pretty hard on us, as it rained a good portion of the time we were on the road.

A rather ludicrous incident happened at the crossing of Fishing Creek. It was raining in torrents at the time, and we were all wet to the skin—all except comrade Jack Culp, whom I have had occasion to mention once before. Jack had by some means managed to get hold of an umbrella and had kept himself tolerable dry until we reached the creek. You may imagine what a figure old Jack cut wading the water almost to his arms carrying an umbrella over his head to keep himself dry. The sight struck u& all as so ridiculous that the whole regiment whooped and yelled, but it made no difference to old Jack. He still clung to his umbrella. The incident had its good results, as it almost made us forget the bitterness of wading the deep and chilling waters.

Another incident that I remember happened here which came near being a sad one.

One of Company "D" boys, I think it was, after wading the creek lay his musket down against a large flat rock that was leaning against the bank near the fence, and sat down on the rock himself for the purpose of emptying the water out of his shoes and wringing out his socks. As he sat down his musket slipped down the rock in such a manner as to pull back the hammer and cause the weapon to be discharged, the ball passing through the tail of his blouse, almost grazing his body and passed very close to his head.

The young fellow was badly frightened, and his face will never be whiter when he lays cold in death than it was at that moment. It is true as the old lady said, "A gun is dangerous without lock, stock or barrel," and a man cannot be too careful when he is handling one.

We were encamped here at Somerset, New Year's Day, the second New Year's for us since we entered the service and the day that has gone down in History as the "Cold New Year's" 1864. I don't think I shall ever forget it while I live and keep my right mind, for it was certainly the coldest day that I ever experienced. There was a great deal of suffering that day in the army. Many of the boys got their feet, hands and ears frozen, but I do not remember that any of the boys at Somerset suffered that way.

Comrade Blizzard and I thought we would try to find a warmer climate than the camp, so we left camp and started out into the country to find a house. I do not know why we did not go into town, but perhaps we were afraid of the patrols. Well, after going about a mile we came to a house, but as it was near one of our picket posts, the guards had possession and were firing up with fence rails or anything else that would burn to keep the women and children from freezing. There were several children and the poor things were blue with cold, for all the boys were firing up pretty strong.

Blizzard and I stopped awhile with them and could have stopped there that night, but we decided to get out and give the women and children a better chance at the fire. We saw no men about except the soldier boys, so we returned to camp and found that a number of our boys had gone down into a large hollow at the mouth of a cave, where there was an old log building, and had built a huge fire and were going to remain there for the night and had left word in camp for us to follow them should we return from our trip in the country. It did not take us long to locate them, and we also found that comrade Jack Culp had been out foraging, and had brought in a sheep so we had mutton for supper, and as the wind could not strike us down in there, we passed the night fairly well.

The boys that remained in camp had huge log heap fires and managed to keep from freezing.

We remained at Somerset until about the third of January, drew ten days' rations and moved down to Burnside Point, crossed over the Cumberland River and went into camp in a pine thicket or grove. I remember yet that the trees were covered with ice and snow. How they glittered when the wintry sun would shine out! The coating of ice that clung to the pine branches sparkled in the sunbeams like diamond jewels. It was indeed a beautiful winter scene, and one I could have enjoyed had my surroundings been different. That is, had the country been at peace and I could have been there simply as a peaceable citizen, studying the beauty of nature, for if one wants to study the beauty of nature, he must see it in the grasp of winter, as well as in the balmy summer. Must see it when hoar frost' has painted the landscape as well as when the flowers are sparkling with the dewdrops of June.

But while we were waiting for better weather and enjoying ourselves in our camp among the pines, we were eating a hole in our ten days' rations, and still had that nine or ten days' march ahead of us over the Cumberland Mountains.

Finally on the 8th day of January, without drawing anymore rations, we broke camp and moved forward, having with us the Ninety-first Indiana Infantry and the Sixth Michigan Battery, all under the command of General Gilbert, and now came the tug of war.

We did not get far till we began to climb the mountains; toward evening, we came to a very steep incline, and to make it still worse, the ground was icy, with a small skiff of snow on top. This made it impossible for the mules to pull the wagons up the hill or mountain, I suppose would be the proper name to give it.

So it became necessary to fasten the ropes of the battery to the wagons and pull them up by hand, and if my memory serves me rightly, part of the wagons, or perhaps all of them, remained at the foot of the hill until the next morning. But I remember the Fiftieth camped on top of the hill, and, oh, what a disagreeable night we passed. The weather was still cold, and the snow and ice hid all the dry wood and as there were no rail fences in sight, we had nothing to build fires with but green pine wood, and if the reader has ever had any experience in trying to kindle a fire with that kind of material, he can judge that we had a worrisome time of it.' There was plenty of smoke, but very little fire, so when morning dawned, we were smoked Yankees sure enough.

I have neglected to mention that our band boys in the past year had furnished themselves with a set of brass instruments, and as they had plenty of time to practice they had become quite proficient and made excellent music.

In the morning after our first night in the mountains, Colonel Strickland posted the band on the brow of the hill, and every wagon we would pull up, the band would play us a nice lively tune that encouraged and kept us in good spirits, and we soon had the wagons all up, and resumed our march.

We went into camp the second day before it got very dark, and we had the good fortune of finding plenty of rich pine knots, and they made splendid fires. While I was busy hunting pine knots, I heard our postmaster (Billy Child) loudly calling my name. Hastening to him, I was agreeably surprised by him handing me a letter from one of my brothers in Ohio. It struck me at the time as something rather odd to receive a letter on top of the Cumberland Mountains.

You may be sure I was delighted to get it, for it reminded me that though I was absent from my loved ones, I was not forgotten, and this thought is always a very comforting one to the young soldier, who is miles away from his old home for the first time in his life.

I kept no journal of this march across the mountains. My impression is that our first day and nights experience was the worst we had, though for that matter it was all bad enough. I thought as I tramped along, how I would enjoy such a trip as this in the good old summer time, when all nature wears her happiest smiles, for one who wishes to live close to nature could enjoy that wish among those rugged mountains to his heart's content. For even when King Winter reigns supreme in these lonely solitudes, one who has the taste and desire to observe closely can trace the handiwork of the All-wise Creator.

We crossed many little mountain streams, whose waters as they murmured along over their gravely bottoms were as clear as crystal, and the borders of those streams were fringed with the mountain laurel, whose leaves remain green summer and winter.

There was at this time some few deer and wild turkeys in these wilds, but they were wild indeed, and it was very seldom that a hunter would get close enough to bring one down with his trusty rifle.

The route we traveled could scarcely be called a road, yet there were landmarks that showed us plainly that other troops and army wagons had traveled this same road before us.

At intervals, we would pass the remains of some poor mule, who had mired down, and been left to perish by the way. Some of the boys called them mile posts, while others would cry out: "Mark him, double duty" Poor, patient mules! It is shameful to think how the innocent beasts were abused and made to suiter during the war; they were starved, whipped, kicked, beat with clubs and cursed, and yet our army would have been at a loss without them.

But many things were done during the war that was cruel, to the soldiers as well as their patient friend, the government mule. True, many of these cruelties could not be avoided, but still there were many things that could have been managed different, and done away with a large amount of suffering, misery and cruelty.

General Sherman has well described war when he said it was hell. But all good and bad earthly things must come to an end, so this mountain trip of ours ended January 16th by easing our wagons down with ropes into Powell's Valley, where we went into camp.

We were nine days making the trip. The distance was said to be seventy-five miles, so we averaged a little over eight miles a day. We ran short of rations, and had to shorten up our belts a few holes each day. Green persimmons were not in season, or we could have eaten some of those, and they would have puckered up our stomachs so that they would not require any food.

ON TO KNOXVILLE

Camp near Jacksboro, Tenn., Jan. 27, 1864.

"This is the first opportunity I have had to write to you all since leaving Somerset. We were there on New Year's Day, and. oh! how cold it was. How was it in Ludlow that day? I hope you all had plenty of wood and coal to burn, for it was a terrible cold day.

"The squad that I bunk with left the camp and went down in a deep hollow at the mouth of a cave, where we found an old log building. In there, the wind could not reach us. We built a huge fire and passed our time very comfortable.

"We remained at Somerset until about the third or fourth of the month. Then drawing ten days' rations, we marched down to Burnside Point and crossed to this side of the Cumberland River. Went into camp in a pine grove. Here we remained till the morning of the eighth, when we broke camp and started on our trip over the mountains. The troops with us were the Ninety-first Indiana and the Sixth Michigan Battery, all under the command of General Gilbert. The weather was cold at the start, and the ground was covered slightly with a coating of ice and snow. In places, the road was so steep, we had to fasten ropes to the cannon and wagons and pull them up by hand. I would love to make this trip in warm weather, but in the winter it is very disagreeable, tramping through these wilds.

"By remaining at the river so long after drawing our rations, we ran out before we got across. We were three days on full rations. Two days on half rations; three days on fourth rations, and one day on no rations at all.

"We were nine days making the trip across. On the evening of the 16th, we reached the jumping off place, and had to use the ropes again, and let our wagons down by hand into the valley, where we are now encamped.

"The Ninety-first Indiana has gone to Cumberland Gap, and the Sixth Michigan Battery to Knoxville, so we are informed. Don't know what became of General Gilbert, but no matter, none of us have much use for him.

Charles Champion Gilbert (1822–1903) was widely despised by the men in his corps for being a martinet. He spent the rest of the war without a battle command.—Ed. 2017

"We arrived here hungry and weary, but not discouraged. Powell's Valley is a rich valley. There was plenty of corn raised here the last season.

"Next morning after our arrival, the teams were sent out to hunt us something to eat. They found plenty of corn and meat. The corn they took to the mills and had it ground into meal. In a day or two everything was running smoothly and we had plenty to eat.

"The weather has become more moderate, and our teams have gone back to Point Burnside after rations for us. In the meantime, we are living off of the country, and are getting fat. I weigh almost two hundred pounds. We eat corn bread and sorghum syrup, corn pork and drink corn coffee. Guess we will soon have to acknowledge the corn.

"Our regiment is at work on a road running back through the mountains. We spend a part of each day on it. I have no idea at present how long we will remain here. Should we stay until we finish the road, it will take some time. We are 35 miles from Knoxville.

"Direct your letters to Knoxville, as all our mail comes by that route. Writing material is very scarce with us here. Write me as often as you can, as you have no idea how it cheers us boys to get news from home.

"Our trip over the mountains was rather hard on us, but we have all got rested up now, and its hardships and privations are forgotten. We were glad to get over into Tennessee, and leave the dark and bloody ground of Kentucky, where we have passed most of our time since we have been in the service."

It was while we were encamped here that I lost one of my chums, Comrade Henry Liebrook. He was stricken down with inflammatory rheumatism, and did not live but a few days. We buried him with honors of war. Poor Henry! he was a good boy, a good soldier, a whole-souled comrade, a very warm friend of mine, and I missed him sadly. He sleeps in old Tennessee, far away from home and loved ones. Peace to his ashes.

When we first arrived here, we had nothing to eat, but Jack Culp came to the rescue of our squad; he made some trade, by which he received several corn cakes that tided us over till we got things into running order. Old Jack thought a great deal of his stomach, and was constantly on the lookout for something to put in it.

We had not been camped here many days until Jack in some of his rambles found out where there was some wild mountain hogs had their rendezvous at night, but they were so wild it was impossible to get near them in the daytime.

So Jack detailed three or four of the boys to go with him, and they left camp one morning before daylight on a still hunt. In an hour or two, they returned, each loaded with fresh pork. Old Jack had made good once more, and we certainly enjoyed the fresh pork with our corn pone and sorghum molasses, and voted Comrade Jack a "Ji Dandy."

Jack and I went out into the valley one day to see if we could buy some butter, and in going up to a farmer's residence we had to pass by his milk house. We saw a nice crock of butter, and we made sure we would have no trouble in purchasing some of it at least. But we were very much disappointed. They positively refused to sell us anything. Somewhat crestfallen, we returned to camp, but on the way we decided if that butter remained in the same place that night we would have it, sell or no sell.

That evening then, a short time after dusk, two boys in blue might have been seen stealing out of camp and skulking through the bushes, so as to avoid the pickets, and making a bee line across Powell's Valley for a certain spring house, which in due time they reached, and notwithstanding the loud barking of the dogs, they entered, but alas! only to find the jar of nice yellow butter missing. We now remembered of meeting one of the officers' cooks with a package in his arms as we came along, and no doubt he was the laddie that got the butter. It was engaged to him, I suppose, was the reason the parties refused to sell it to Jack and me in the morning. Well, we had to acknowledge we were beat, but we made the best we could of a bad bargain. We drank all the sweet milk we could hold and then took one of the milk jars to camp with us. It came in quite handy to mix our corn meal batter in, and we used it for that purpose while we remained at this camp.

I wish to relate something now that I fear will place comrade Culp in a position where his good qualities will not shine as bright as I could wish them to, but I promised myself when I commenced writing these reminiscences that I would try to hew to the line let the chips fall where they would, and so far, I have kept that promise, and I still intend to hold to it, though it should put me in a bad light myself.

I am afraid I have to some extent strained my reputation already, but old veteran readers all know from experience that it was hard for a soldier to always keep his conduct and character unspotted.

But now for the incident. Comrades Jack Culp and Sergeant Sam Lousy went one afternoon on a private scout of their own, and getting interested talking to the ladies they met at different houses, as soldiers naturally would, they got belated and night overtook them a mile or so from camp. On the way, they had to pass a house where two ladies and some children lived.

Jack knocked on the door, but got no response, as there happened to be no one at home just at that time. Jack says, "Let's go in and see what we can find"; Lousy says, "No, come on, let's go to camp," but Jack bolted in, and Sam, after going on a few steps, stopped and waited until Jack overtook him. Jack told Sam then that he had taken two tin cups, a book and a molasses canister. Now I can't say whether Jack knew what kind of a book it was when he was taking it or not, but when he got into camp and to a light, it proved to be a small family Bible with the family record in it.

Next morning we ate the molasses out of the canister, and Jack threw the canister in the fire and burnt it up, and took the cups and Bible and hid them in the leaves and brush on top of our shanty.

Just about that time the women made their appearance in camp, and went to Colonel Strickland and reported the theft; they said they cared for nothing but the Bible, but as that had their family record in, they would like to have it back. Colonel Strickland had the camp searched, but of course no Bible was found. By the way, the women had seen Culp and Lousy that afternoon they were out, and said they were almost positive that they were the ones that had entered their house and stolen their Bible.

The Colonel asked them if they could identify the men if they saw them again. They said they thought they could. So the Colonel had the regiment ordered into line, but the women failed to identify the culprits. Then Colonel Strickland made us a short speech, and the way he went for the man that took that Bible was something fierce. He finally said he hoped whoever the man was that he would take the Bible and turn to the Ten Commandments and read them, as he thought it would benefit him to do so. He then dismissed us to our quarters.

We boys that were in Jack's squad—or mess, as we soldiers called it—told Jack he ought to return the Bible, for he had done very wrong to take it, and we advised him to return it, but he seemed to feel so ashamed and guilty of what he had done, he hesitated and refused to do so.

I then proposed that he would allow Lousy and me to return it; he readily consented to this proposition. So Lousy and I took the Bible and tin cups and returned them to the ladies. They were highly pleased to get their Bible back and were very profuse in thanking us for the interest and trouble we had taken for them, and readily agreed to drop the incident and make no further trouble for Jack. They became quite friendly to Lousy and I, and we dropped in on them several times after that, and passed some pleasant hours with them.

On one of our calls we had the pleasure of meeting two young ladies from up in the mountains, and they were as pretty as pictures; their lips were the color of ripe May cherries, and their cheeks had the beautiful pink blush of the Hermose rose; they were charming, but were rather shy in the presence of us boys in blue. Lousy and I were badly smitten with them, but, alas! before we had the pleasure of meeting them a second time, we were ordered to Knoxville, and never saw our mountain pinks

We often regretted that the fates were so cruel to us, but perhaps it may have been all for the best. We stayed rather late the night we met them, and as we were crossing a large, level meadow on the way to camp, we were somewhat startled to see two lights a short way in front of us, that at first we took to be lanterns, carried by two persons, but after watching them closely for awhile, we became convinced they were phantom lights, or what are generally called "jack-o-lanterns." They looked to be about three or four feet from the ground, and they traveled first in one direction and then another, and seemed to wander around, as though they were hunting for something, and although we now understood what they were, yet they had an uncanny appearance, and caused a creepy sensation to crawl slowly up our spinal columns, and we could feel the hair on our heads gradually assume an upright position, much like the hair of a cat's back when it is badly frightened, and our caps were elevated until we had to readjust them to keep them on our heads.

But finally we reached the woods beyond the lights, and with many a backward glance over our shoulders to see if they were following us, we arrived at camp in safety.

It was while at this camp I received the discouraging news that "one of the girls I left behind me," and with whom I had been corresponding, growing tired of waiting for me to come home to claim her, concluded to marry one of the stay-at-home guards, and I understood the last letter I wrote to her was handed her a few minutes after she became a bride.

This was the second one of my young lady correspondents to marry since I had entered the service, but being a strong believer in the old saying that the third time is the charm, I soon opened up a correspondence with a young lady that had been a schoolmate of mine, and we continued to correspond until the close of the war and I had returned home, but sad to relate, she took sick and died in a short time after my return.

But such is life. Here in this world, we meet many disappointments; things will not always come our way, and it is well we are so constituted as to soon forget our troubles and disappointments; our lives are to a large extent built upon hopes for the future.

We no sooner see one of our idols that we have taken such care to rear shattered, than we begin in our imagination to rear others, and hope to be more fortunate in the future.

Thus it was with Lousy and I. We felt cruelly disappointed in not being permitted to meet our mountain pinks but the one time; yet we soon forgot their, smiling faces, sparkling eyes and rosy cheeks, and began to peer into the future, hoping we might have better luck next time.

We remained at this camp perhaps four or five weeks, put in four or six hours each day, working on a road back through Wheeler's Gap.

When our teams returned from Burnside Point with supplies for us, we were ordered to Knoxville, where we went into camp on the south side of the river, on a hill overlooking the city of Knoxville. Here we had a beautiful camp laid off, and took young cedar and pine trees and bordered all our streets. The wind had a fair chance at us, so we had plenty of fresh air.

There were some Ohio heavy artillery men in Fort Sanders on the opposite side of the river from us, and some of Company "K" boys paid them a visit one day, and found in their ranks two men that had deserted from Company "K" some months before.

When the boys brought the word back to camp that they had found the deserters. Lieutenant Pine sent over a file of men and arrested them, and had them brought back to the company. Poor fellows, I suppose they were afraid to stay home, and were afraid to come back to the regiment after being away so long, and not knowing what else to do, they enlisted in the Heavy Artillery, little dreaming, I suppose, that they would ever see the old Fiftieth again, but it seemed to be so ordered that they become, as it were, our next-door neighbors.

After laying around camp awhile under arrest, they were put on duty, and became good soldiers; one of them met his death afterwards at the Battle of Franklin, Tennessee.

While at Knoxville, I received word that my mother was lying very sick, and was not expected to live.

Lieutenant Pine at once wrote me out a furlough, and Colonel Strickland approved it, but when it was presented to General

Scofield he wrote on it, "Disapproved," "For the present." That settled the furlough business with me, but at the time I was afraid I would never see my mother again this side of eternity, but I am glad to say she got well again, and lived to see the close of the war, and she had the joy and happiness of welcoming her soldier boy home again.

There was at Knoxville at this time a camp of soldiers, composed, I will say, of odds and ends of different regiments. They were a tough set—all guilty, I presume, of some wrongdoing, as they were kept under guard, and made to work on the fortifications. Our boys did not crave the job of standing guard over them. I am glad to say I escaped that very unpleasant duty.

"Knoxville, Tennessee, March 24th, 1864.

"Beloved Parents:

"I seat myself this morning for the purpose of conversing a short time with you through the medium of the pen. I always esteem it a pleasure to devote some of my leisure; moments in thus conversing with those who watched over me in my infancy, and on up till I reached the verge of manhood.

"I often think of how far short I have come of repaying you for all the worry and care you have bestowed on me in the past; not only that, but when I have been standing on the lonely picket post, or lying awake in my tent in the long hours of the night, my mind had wandered back to many little acts of mine that had caused you sorrow and pain.

"Sometimes these things were done in the heat of passion; at others, they were done thoughtlessly on my part, and while I know that long ago you have forgiven me, and blotted them from your memories, yet the knowledge that I was guilty of them rankles in my heart like a thorn in the flesh.

"O! if I only could live over my boyhood days with the knowledge that I have now, what a different life I would live, but the past cannot be recalled. I can only improve the present, and whatever little of the future God shall see proper in His wisdom to permit me to enjoy, God help me to improve the talent and the time he allots me to live a better life, shall be my constant prayer.

"And I know that your prayers ascend up daily to a throne of grace, asking that a Heavenly Father's protecting care shall be thrown around me, and this knowledge shall strengthen me to meet the temptations and trials along the pathway of life with a brave and unfaltering courage.

"I received your letter of the 13th yesterday, and was agreeably surprised to find it filled with writing material, of which I have been sadly in need for the past month; but our wants were all relieved on the 19th by the arrival of the long-looked-for paymaster, who paid us four months' pay. Out of this I sent you forty dollars. This was the best I could do for you at this time. Keep in good heart.

"Down here a great many of the citizens draw all they eat from Uncle Sam, but I hope you have not come to that point yet.

"The Fiftieth is camped at present south of the Tennessee River on a high hill, overlooking the city of Knoxville.

"Colonel Strickland is in command of all the troops on this side of the river. We are still at our old employment, building fortifications.

"We have a nice camp here; we have our streets all bordered with evergreen trees, which gives it a very cheerful appearance. We draw full rations, so have no complaints to make in that line. We are all fat and 'sassy' as young bucks.

"We are building two forts here that will be hard for the Johnnies to take if they remain away till we get them finished. Here is hoping they will never get back here in force again.

"They did have General Burnside in close quarters here at one time, but our boys bravely stood them off until Longstreet heard that Uncle Billy was on the way here; then he thought it was time for him to crawfish, so he backed into Virginia.

"Day before yesterday snow fell here the depth of six inches, but it has about all disappeared, only in the mountains. Last night, though, was a real cold night; the ground froze solid, but it will soon be April now; then we can begin to look for better weather.

"We are now said to be in the Fourth Division, Third Brigade, Twenty-third Corps. A tell-a-lie-gram over the grapevine says Twenty-third Corps is ordered to Texas, but I think we will go to Georgia before many days, for trouble is brewing down there for somebody, if I don't mistake my guess.

"Thanking you all for writing material and your kind letter, I close for this time.

"I remain as ever. Your affectionate son,

"Erastus Winters."

WRITER STRIKES A SOFT SNAP

"Loudon, Tennessee, April 17th, 1864.

"You will see by the heading of this letter the Fiftieth has changed camping grounds once more. Yes, we left Knoxville the 15th, and arrived here yesterday. We found some fine-looking farms on the way here, but the most of them are lying idle. It made me feel sad to look at them.

"We begin to get down now where we can see the effects of the war. Pleasant homes have been broken up; farms have been deserted; fences and other property destroyed.

"People of the North would hardly know a war was going on if they did not miss those who are in the service; but down here the war has been brought right to their doors, where they cannot only see but feel its blighting influence.

"God speed the day when the White Dove of Peace shall once more hover over our beloved land.

"I am glad that mother is improving. I trust she will be fully restored to her usual health again.

"Many thanks are due to Mrs. William Childs, the wife of our postmaster, as she always writes some word from you people to her husband. It was through her kindness that I first learned of mother's improvement.

"I wanted to get home during her illness very bad, but General Scofield would not grant me that privilege, but I am perfectly satisfied that you were all kind to her, and if good nursing would restore her to health, I expect to hear she has fully recovered, for I know she has had the best of care.

"She has been a kind and affectionate mother to me, and I trust I shall have the pleasure of meeting her once more this side of the grave.

"I have been very busy today, building a house to live in. It is not quite finished yet, but I am going to sleep in it tonight. We are camped near the railroad bridge that crosses the Tennessee River at this place. They are building a new bridge, as the old one had been destroyed; they have it about completed; trains are now crossing it.

From appearances, it looks like we might stay here for some time; still we are so near the front now, we are likely to be sent there at any time."

"Loudon, April 24th, 1864.

"Dear Sister:

"Your letter reached me on the 22nd; glad to hear you are all in as good circumstances as you are; very happy to hear mother is so far on the road to recovery, and so you want me to write you a big letter.

"Well, I will do my best. I think I am rather a poor hand to write letters. Maybe when I have had more practice, I will do better.

"We had a nice shower of rain here this morning, after which it cleared off warm and pleasant. We have had a great deal of rain down here this spring, and a great deal of cold, disagreeable weather also, but it seems to be more settled now, and I trust we will have fine weather from now on.

"We have the prettiest camp here we have ever had yet. I wish you could see it. We are right on the bank of the Tennessee River, about five hundred yards from where the new railroad bridge spans it. We can see the steamboats and cars passing every day. That looks a little more like living than it did in Wheeler's Gap, Cumberland Mountains.

"The ground where we are camped is very gravelly; it makes no difference how much rain falls, it will never be muddy. We have nice little houses to live in; they are just large enough for four men to room in. Take it all in all, we are fixed very nice for soldiers.

"Loudon is not much of a town; it is not quite as large as Ludlow, Ky., but has got plenty of room to grow, and likely will grow after the war is over, for some of the boys in blue will no doubt come back here and settle when peace is declared.

"One thing Tennessee can boast of is her pretty girls, and many of them, I am sure, are so attractive that they will draw many a Yankee boy back here.

"James Lacey, of whom you wrote in your letter, never came back to the company. I do not know what became of him. William Sparks also deserted us, while we were at Lebanon, Kentucky, and has never returned.

"Lieutenant Pine is at present on detached duty at Knoxville. Lieutenant Anderson is in command of Company "K" at this writing.

"It surprised me to hear of so many weddings since I entered the service. I am really afraid all the girls will be married before I get back. Can't you persuade some of them to wait for me? Tell them it's only seventeen months; that is not long. Surely some of them will take pity on me, and wait. But what surprised me most was to hear you speak of getting married. Is it possible that my little sister has grown so fast? No wonder you write I would not know you. It astonished me, but I suppose it is true, or you would not say so, but you must not marry till I get home, for I want to be at your wedding. Give my regards to Mr. Sweet, and Mr. Harris, and tell them to write to me, for I do love to get letters; they are the golden links that bind me to the dear ones at home. Without them my life in the army would be a desolate blank—a sort of barren desert.

"I enclose you a song entitled, 'What's a Home Without Sister?' That, I think, is very appropriate.

"Well, sister, it is after taps; I must close for this time. Write soon to your soldier brother. Good night."

"Loudon, Tennessee, May 14th, 1864."

"Well, I have struck a pretty soft job down here. I am on what might be called detached duty. I have three men with me, and we are guarding a lot of horses and mules in pasture at the mouth of Sweet Water Creek on the Tennessee River, three miles from camp.

"We are having a regular picnic; lots of pretty girls down here, and fishing and talking with the girls is the order of the day at my headquarters. The boys in camp are having it pretty hard; they go on guard about every other day. There is only the Fiftieth Ohio and the Fourth Tennessee Infantry, one company of cavalry and a battery of artillery, so it makes the duty pretty severe.

"This is a fine farming country here, but the people appear to be poor farmers; the majority of them break up their land with shovel plows, so you may imagine what kind of crops they produce. To tell the truth, there are not many able-bodied men here. The women do most of the farm work. It is no strange sight down here to see young girls hauling rails or wood, or plowing in the fields.

"The able-bodied men are in the army, either on one side or the other, but my impression is that the majority of the people in this part of Tennessee were loyal. They have been driven from their homes, and many of them found their way over the Cumberland Mountains and entered the Union army; others were caught, and pressed into the rebel army, and still a few others, whose sympathy was with the South, have joined the rebel army of their own free will. This happened, of course, before the Union army got in here.

"As a class, the loyal Tennesseans have suffered more during the war thus far than any other class, and I assure you, seeing what I have seen around here, they have my individual sympathy. Talk about your sunny South—here it is the 4th of May, and for two nights now we have had heavy frost, and although I rolled up head and ears in my woolen blanket, I slept cold; however, it has cleared off warm now, and the beautiful sun is shining bright and spring like. It makes me feel real good to see it. Maybe we have had our last frost this spring.

"I understand there is fighting going on at Dalton. Ga. I think it is likely Sherman has opened up the spring campaign. If he has, you may look out for stirring news from that quarter right along.

"I was sorry to hear of the death of Mr. Collins and his daughter. Poor Lide, she did not live long to enjoy her married life. (By the way, this Miss Collins was one of the girls I left behind me, and was the first one of my correspondents to marry after I entered the service.) But it is a road we must all travel, sooner or later. Life is uncertain, but death is sure.

"Lide was a good girl, and I trust she has entered into that blessed home where sickness, sorrow, pain and death are unknown, and where there is eternal happiness and peace.

"These lines leave me in good health. May they reach you in safety, and find you all enjoying the same blessing."

We had not been at Loudon but a few days until the writer and three men were detailed and sent out in the country about three miles to look after a lot of horses and mules that were on pasture in a large field on Sweet Water Creek. We were quartered in a log house on the bank of the creek, a few hundred yards from where it emptied into the Tennessee River. Our duty was very light; we did not have to stand guard. We simply counted the horses and mules nights and mornings, and salted them every two or three days; in fact, I never saw much need of us being there, for anyone could have driven the animals all away any night, and we would have known nothing about it till morning, as we were told we need not post any guards. So we had what we boys called a soft snap. Our house stood in the midst of a field of clover, and as the weather began to get pleasant the clover sprang up, and as there were plenty of groundhogs along the banks of the creek, they would come out to play and feed on the young clover, and we had fine sport shooting them. We also cooked and ate them, and we considered them very good eating.

There was a small piece of woods near us, and we killed several squirrels there. That made us fine eating, and we also did a good deal of fishing in the river, and had fairly good luck. Besides these, some of our good neighbors furnished us with sweet milk for our coffee. So adding all these extras to Uncle Sam's rations, we thought we were living at the top of the notch for soldiers.

I formed the acquaintance of quite a number of people here, and they were very sociable, and appeared to be Unionists, and I believe the most of them were. I think I met one gentleman here that had served as Major in the Union army, but I cannot recall his name.

As I have stated before, about all of the able-bodied men were in the service, but there were plenty of women and young ladies. The poor women and girls had to do the men's work. I saw them hauling rails and wood, and doing other farm work. I had never seen women doing that kind of work when I was at home, so you may be sure it looked strange to me to see them driving team, doing the work that I had always seen men and boys do. But with them it was a case of necessity, and they took up their burdens as cheerfully as could be expected under the circumstances.

There was an old gentleman and his two daughters lived quite near where we camped. One of the daughters was married, and had a little boy, perhaps three or four years of age. The woman's husband was a soldier in the Union army. We all became quite intimate with this family; they were nice, clever people, and were very kind to us while we remained here. The little boy and I were quite chummy. The little fellow would call out, "How do, Mr. Winters," or "I see you, Mr. Winters," whenever he caught sight of me. The other boys tried to run the joke on me, about the boy, of course, but I attended to my business, and let them laugh. I am sorry that I have forgotten those good people's names, but it is a pleasure for me to say that their kindly acts of charity toward me are still fresh in my memory, and the hearty welcome they gave me in their humble home reminded me of my own, far away in Ludlow, Kentucky.

Among the families I became acquainted with here was one by the name of Grammer, consisting of father, mother, son and three daughters, though the son was absent at the time in the Confederate army.

This was the family of George Washington Grammer and Ruth Boothe. The son in the army was Benjamin, who survived the war. There were actually five sisters, Eliza, Phebe, Mary, Margaret, and Sarah.—Ed. 2017

The sisters were named Eliza, Phebe and Mary. Miss Phebe was slightly crippled, having fallen from a horse at some period early in life; all three of the girls were sociable and fine looking.

Now grammar as a study had always been a very distasteful branch of study for me, but now all at once, it became very interesting to me, and I was really surprised to find how very fascinating the study proved, if one placed their whole mind on it. So it is needless to say that I took up that branch of study at once, and pursued it with zeal, and found that the harder I studied, and the longer the lessons, the better it pleased me. The sisters were splendid teachers, and they found me a promising pupil.

Small wonder then, that I, surrounded as I was here by the refining influence of those three beautiful sisters, and with nature just awakening from her winter's sleep, the warm spring sunshine causing the brown meadows to array themselves in their robes of green, and the flowers and orchards to burst into bloom, filling the air with their delightful fragrance, while the birds, their bright plumage flashing in the sunlight, as they flitted from branch to branch among the sweet bloom of the apple and cherry, praising the great Creator those bright, beautiful, pure May mornings with their happy songs—small wonder, I repeat that I, surrounded as I was here in this peaceful valley with such pleasant associations, should forget for the time being that a wicked rebellion was in progress, and that I was one among many that had promised Uncle Sam that I would use my best efforts to try and put it down.

But such was the case, and I was rudely awakened from my peaceful-slumbers on the morning of the 17th of May by a messenger from Colonel Strickland, with an order for me to report with my men to regimental headquarters, at Loudon immediately, as we were ordered to Cleveland, Tennessee.

Thus again was one of my dreams of happiness brought to an abrupt close. Partaking of a hasty breakfast, we gathered up our traps, and bidding our many friends a sorrowful good bye, we hastened to headquarters.

Goodbye and farewell. What sad words those are! How it makes our hearts ache sometimes when it falls to our lot to say them. So it was with me that May morning in old Tennessee, as I said good bye to my little boy chum, his mother, aunt and grandfather.

My mind and heart was filled with sad thoughts, and sadder, and still more bitter, was the parting with my good friends, the Grammers. for I had become very much interested in them, and had hoped that I might be permitted to pass at least a portion of the summer in this delightful valley; had I been granted that privilege, I am sure I would have improved my time and talents, and with such interesting teachers, who can say what the results might have been, but Fate ordered it otherwise.

I was suddenly brought back from the land of dreams in which I had been reveling, to face the stern reality that I was still a soldier for Uncle Sam, and it was his will I was expected to obey, and not my own.

However, I was not deprived of my lessons entirely, for I continued them by mail while in the service, and for several months after the close of the war, and found it both interesting and enjoyable. The young ladies gave me a pressing invitation to visit them after I returned home.

Said they would make me a big party, and assured me I would have a good time, if I would come, but I failed to accept the invitation. They also informed me their brother had returned home. He had been a member of the Texas Cavalry.

Forty years have rolled by into the fading past since those eventful days, and just a few days ago, I received a letter from Mr. Grammer, the brother, and he informs me that his sisters all married, and are now living at Harriman, Tennessee. The father and mother long ago passed over the dark River. Mr. Grammer and his sisters like myself are growing old.

It is not likely that we will ever meet again in this world, but I trust I shall meet, and strike hands with them under the shade of the Tree of Life, on the shore of the Mystic River, where no farewells will ever be spoken.

Glancing backward over the departing years to those days, when my whole being was in harmony with the delicious spring weather, there comes floating to me through the mist, sweet memories of the pleasant hours I passed so happily on the banks of the beautiful Tennessee.

"Cleveland, Tennessee, May 19th, 1864.

"I drop you these few lines that you may know my present whereabouts.

"On the 17th, six companies of the Fiftieth boarded the cars at Loudon and came down to this pleasant little town, and today the other four companies arrived.

"Oh! how disappointed I was when I learned I must give up my delightful situation I had in Sweet Water Valley. I had just become well enough acquainted in the neighborhood to make it interesting to me, and if I could have remained there this summer, I would have had the time of my life. Still, it is useless to mourn over blasted hopes, but I shall always treasure the memories of the few happy days passed there, as an interesting page in my life's history.

"Cleveland is a very pretty little town, situated on the Knoxville & Loudon railroad, but our stay here is very short. We leave here in the morning for the front, where they are fighting now every day.

"Dalton, Georgia, is twenty-eight miles from here, and the army is twenty-two miles beyond that. Uncle Billy has opened up the spring campaign, and is crowding General Johnson back.

"You may expect exciting war news from Georgia from now on.

Some of our line officers have been very anxious to go to the front for quite a while; guess they will get all the front they want in a few days. I trust if the little Fiftieth gets into trouble, she will give a good account of herself. Will write again as soon as possible. I know not what the future has in store for me, but I shall, as I always have, put my trust in my Heavenly Father, who is able to protect me, for not a sparrow falls to the ground without His notice."

THE ATLANTA CAMPAIGN.

On March 2, 1864, Lincoln promoted Ulysses S. Grant to lieutenant general (reviving the rank last held by George Washington), giving him command of all Union Armies, answering only to the President. The Atlanta Campaign, led by General William Tecumseh Sherman ran throughout the spring and summer of 1864.—Ed. 2017

On the morning of the 20th of May, 1864, the fiftieth Ohio flung her banner to the breeze, and stepped off toward the firing line, which was then somewhere near Kingston, Georgia. [About 56 miles/90 km northwest of Atlanta.]

The weather was extremely warm for May, and the boys being a little soft from laying in camp so long, suffered accordingly.

Colonel Strickland being a bit out of humor, marched us pretty hard, so hard, in fact, that the surgeon of the Regiment, called him down, and told him if he continued at that pace, he would kill all the boys before they reached the front. After that, he took a somewhat slower step.

It will be impossible for me in these reminiscences to recall all the places that the 50th Ohio were in, or to name the different moves we made, and the day and dates for the same, as I kept no memorandum during the campaign.

I will, however, give the most important moves and skirmishes that we took a part in, and this I will do partly from memory, and partly from letters that I wrote home at the time. But I will say just here that from the time we reached the front, the 27th or 28th of May until the fall of Atlanta, the 1st of September, with the exception of two of three days, we were continually under fire, and a good portion of the time, we were on the firing line.

We were assigned to the Third Brigade, Second Division, Twenty-third Corps. The Corps was commanded by General Scofield; the Division by General Haschall; the Brigade by Colonel Strickland; and the Regiment by Lieutenant Colonel Elsner. Our position as a general thing was on the right or left flanks of the army. It seemed to be our luck as a regiment to miss all the main battles of the campaign.

We would be in hearing of them, and sometimes in sight of them; still I will have to admit that we were in some pretty sharp brushes, where the leaden hail came thick and fast, and the shrieking shells got in their deadly work; and as for skirmish fighting, I sincerely believe we did our full share.

We did what we were called on to do; went where our officers ordered us to go, and were never driven out of a position after taking it from the enemy, and I want to say we took some positions from them on this campaign that it required nerve and "bull-dog grit" to hold.

Skirmish fighting often requires as great courage, and stubborn staying qualities, as it does to face a line of glistening steel, or face death by charging a battery of death dealing guns.

While it is true, skirmishers have the right to shield themselves behind trees, stumps, logs or any other object that presents itself to them, yet in advancing on the foe through open fields, very seldom anything of that kind comes in the way, there is only the body of the soldier to stop the ball of the deadly sharpshooter, or to arrest the progress of the ragged fragments of the bursting shells.

And a soldier must also be well blessed with courage and grit to advance through the woods and underbrush, where he knows his enemy is concealed behind some tree, ready to put a minnie ball through his body on sight.

So I would always prefer an enemy I can see, while advancing on them than one than that is hidden.

But now to resume, we finally reached the front, and were placed on the firing line; a rather new experience for us, and we found it quite different from guarding railroad bridges back in Kentucky and Tennessee.

On the way here, we got a look at Buzzard Roost, Snake Creek Gap and Rocky Face Ridge, where there had been severe fighting a few days before. It was a wild looking country, one well adapted by nature for defense, and we could not help being surprised that the Confederates would give up such positions without greater struggle.

From now on, I shall copy quite freely from letters that I sent home during the campaign.

"Near Dallas, Ga., May 31st, 1864.

"Dear Parents, Brothers and Sisters:—

"I suppose you are all anxious to hear from me, so I take the first opportunity that has presented itself since leaving Cleveland, Tennessee, of writing to you.

"We have been so busy dodging rebel bullets and digging trenches, we have had no time to write letters.

"We left Cleveland on the 20th of May, and came on to Cass Station, Georgia, where we had a little fracas with [Joseph] Wheeler's Cavalry. That did not amount to much, and then we came on here, where Ave arrived on the 28th, and took position on the front line, where we still remain.

"Our position is behind breastworks in the woods with a second line in our rear. There is heavy picket or skirmish firing in our front continually.

"We are lying behind a strong breastwork, which we have to hug pretty close, as the balls from the rebel pickets are whizzing over our heads at all hours day and night.

"This morning, the enemy's pickets drove in our pickets all along our front, and came up almost to our works. We raised up, and gave them a volley or two from our main line. That stopped them.

"Colonel Elsney then called on Company "K" to drive them back. We deployed along our regimental front, and at the word of command, we jumped over the works, and went for them. They fired on us as we made the leap, but their aim was bad; they did not hit a man at that time. We had the advantage of them now, and Ave made them hump back where they came from. We came on them behind trees and logs loading their guns.

"There were several of the enemy killed and wounded, and a few prisoners taken.

"John Ponder of Company 'K' was killed out in the woods after we had driven the rebels back to their places, and Company "K" called in again.

"Colonel Elsner complimented Company "K" very highly for what they did. A squad of four or five men of Co. "K" volunteered to go out, and bring in the body of Comrade Pouder, but just as they were ready to pick him up, one of their number (John Klotter) was shot in the neck, so they gathered up Klotter, and brought him in. He lived only a few minutes after he was brought back.

"Joseph Corton was knocked out by a spent ball, but he will be O. K. in a few days.

"William Dean was wounded yesterday while on picket; the doctor says he will get well. Corson and Dean are both from Co. "K".

"Our regimental loss so far is six killed, and fifteen wounded. The rebs have a strong position here, but Sherman will soon flank them out of it, as he has done several times already.

"I am very thankful that my life has been spared thus far. I put my trust in God, and feel confident that he will bring me safely through. I know that I have your prayers, and that encourages and strengthens me. I am in good health and spirits. Will write whenever I have the opportunity. Want you to do the same. Direct to Co. K, O. V. L, 2 Division, 3 Brigade, 23 Corps, Kingston, Georgia. I close now with my best wishes for you all."

This place that we were in the line here was a dangerous one for the picket line; it was in the woods, and the underbrush was very thick.

I was on post here one day, and we all stood behind trees, and fired at the smoke of each other's guns; the tree that fell to my lot was not large enough to hide my body entirely, and I suppose some Johnnie caught sight of the blue behind it, for the way the bullets rained about that tree soon convinced me that if I ever expected to see Cincinnati again, I would have to hunt a larger tree at once.

The tree was about twelve inches through. I was lying flat on the ground with my head behind it. I would lie on my back and load, and turn on my breast, watch for a puff of smoke, and then fire at it, but they got my range down too fine for me.

One of their bullets brushed the leaves within three inches of my right limb, the full length of it. So I began to look for a safer position. A little to my left and rear, I espied a large stump, of which I soon took possession, but did not feel a great deal safer there, for some poor fellow had got his death there, or been badly wounded, as there was a large pool of blood behind it; however, I stuck to the stump until I was relieved.

It would have been safer back of the Ohio River most anywhere than it was in that woods, so we all thought at that particular time.

We moved from here the evening after Comrade Pouder was killed, so we did not recover his body; it lay in a very exposed position. We learned that the troops that relieved us recovered the body that night, and buried it, but I am not able to say positive whether this was true or not.

"June 5th, 1864.

"On the 2nd of June, our brigade drove the rebs back on the left flank three miles. The 50th was in the reserve that day. The 14th Kentucky of our brigade was in front; they met with a small loss. The 14th Kentucky is a splendid regiment. Colonel Gallop commands it; they were mustered into the service, I understand, in 1861.

"We keep driving and flanking the enemy every day; they have strong positions, but when we get around their flank, and begin to threaten their rear, they get up and hustle for another position. I don't mean to say that all our forces have been as lucky as we, for there has been heavy fighting a mile or so to our left and right, but we were not in the muss.

"Where we are down here, we can be in hearing of a big' battle, and still not be in it ourselves. At the same time, we are just as liable to be in the thickest of it as any other regiment.

"Yesterday, our Division was all on the front line, but we have just been relieved; sent to the rear for a day or two's rest we have been on the front line nine days and nights. We slept on our arms in the trenches; the crack of the musket on the skirmish line was continuous. Guess we will enjoy a little rest."

"June 30th, 1864.

"There has been some very hard fighting down here, but no general engagement as yet. Sherman so far, has flanked the enemy out of their strong positions. Nothing makes the Johnnies pull up stakes and travel as quick as to threaten their rear, or as we term it, "Fire end-ways at them".

"A Southern lady told Colonel Elsner the other day that we did not fight fair. Said she, 'Yu all come up in our front, four lines deep, and Are a few shots to draw we'ens' attention, and then send Scofield with his company around, and are end-ways at we'ens'. She seemed to think that was very unfair.

"I suppose you think I ought to be able to tell you just how the army is situated here. Well, if I was a general, perhaps I could, as it would be my business then to know all about it, and my duty would call me from one end of the line of battle to the other, but being a high private in the rear rank, my duty is to stay close to my company, not knowing what moment we may be called into action.

"So you see I have no chance of knowing what is taking place on the other part of the line, and I can't see no distance, for our place is, generally speaking, in the woods and bushes.

"A battle may take place on our right or left, and all the knowledge we would have of it, would be the thunder of the guns, and the rattle of the musketry.

"So you can now understand that in this wilderness, a soldier can see nothing only what transpires in his immediate vicinity. The Fiftieth Regiment is now in the front line, and has been for about ten days. We are lying behind a good line of rifle pits, and about three hundred yards in front is the Confederate line of works, while between, are the two lines of skirmishers, who keep up almost a continuous musket fire on each other, and I write this with the minnie balls whizzing over my head. It becomes very monotonous at times.

"The 14th Kentucky is doing the picket duty in our brigade front at present. Last night, there was no firing done by the pickets; the Yanks and Johnnies got to talking together. Our boys asked them what regiment they belonged to; they answered back, the 37th Georgia. Our boys invited them over, and this morning early, five of them came over, and gave themselves up; they seemed pleased to get out of the scrape. Hardly a day passes but some of them come over, and surrender to our boys.

"It is reported the rebs made a charge on our works last night two miles to our left, but were repulsed with a loss of three hundred; whether true or not, I can't say positive. The rebs had church out in our front last night. We could hear them preaching, singing and praying."

"July 2nd, 1864"

"The night I wrote the first part of this letter, we moved to the rear about one mile. Yesterday we moved to the extreme right of our line; found the rebs in small force, and pushed them back about three miles. They threw a few vicious shells at us, but hurt no one in our regiment. The weather is extremely hot; there were fifteen or sixteen cases of sunstroke in our division yesterday.

"I still keep in very good health. The mail is ready to go out, so I close with my best wishes to one and all."

A good deal of rain fell during the first part of this campaign, and the weather was very hot and sultry, so that when we were advancing or marching to a new position, we suffered from the heat of the sun, and when it rained, it made it very disagreeable for us.

The position of the 23 Corps was mostly on the flank. In taking a new position, if we found the enemy, we would push them back until we got our line where we wanted it, and then we would build breastworks.

I remember one day we pushed the enemy off of a high hill, and formed our lines, captured some of their pickets. We took our position at the edge of a woods with a cleared field in front of us, and at the other side of the field, we could see the breastworks of the rebs as soon as we formed our lines; they began to shell us from three directions.

We lay down in the woods, and there was a detail made from each company to build works in our front. The workers had men to watch; whenever they would see a puff of smoke, the watchers would cry out, "Lie down". When the shell would pass over or burst, they would all jump up and go to work again. They kept this up for perhaps an hour or longer, and then they ceased firing. We had no batteries in position to answer them.

When the firing ceased, General Haschall of our division rode along the lines, and talked to us boys like a father. We all expected the rebs to charge us, and that's what the General thought, and that's what he was talking to us about, telling us what he wanted us to do in case they did.

But much to our surprise everything remained quiet after the shelling was over. We worked nearly all night, and built good solid works, and as they could rake our works end-ways with one of their guns, each company built works to protect their right flank. It was a nasty place to stay while the shelling was going on, as there were 14 or 15 men killed and wounded in the Fiftieth.

In this little fracas, Company "K" had one man wounded in the hand; he lost three fingers of his right hand; his thumb and forefinger was all that remained. His name was Vincent Brislear. He was an Italian, and lived in Cincinnati. He soon received an honorable discharge, and came home.

I had often thought had the rebels known the damage they were inflicting on us, they would have kept up their shelling. Several men were hurt by falling limbs that were cut off by the shells over our heads, where we lay in line in the woods.

But we stuck to the position we had gained, so stubbornly, I suppose, they thought they were doing us no harm, and were only wasting their shells, so they ceased to pitch them at us.

One hot morning in June, we were rushed forward in almost double quick time, and went into line of battle on the right flank of General [Joseph] Hooker's line. I took a severe pain in my head on the road; I suppose I got too hot, as I never had any trouble with my head before.

When we reached our position, I went to our regimental doctor, and wanted him to give me something to relieve me, but he said, 'My boy, I have nothing to do you any good whatever; you best go back there where the band boys are, and lie down in the shade and rest.' I took his advice, and went back and lay down, while the boys on the line went to work, and threw up a line of breastworks.

After resting awhile, I concluded I would go up where the Company was. I had just got up to the Company when Hades broke loose out in our front. We were in the woods as usual. The 14th Kentucky of our brigade was out in front, and for a few minutes there was as lively music as I ever heard.

There was a section of artillery just behind me, and the officer in charge stood behind me watching the effect of their shells. He had his hand resting on my back, or rather he was rubbing my back, while he gave orders to his men about timing their shells.

As soon as the 14th Kentucky fell back into the main line, we raised up, and let the Johnnies have it hot and heavy; they got pretty close to our works, but we made it too hot for them; they went back as fast as they came, and those cannon in our rear almost raised me clear off the ground at every discharge.

There was a ravine run parallel with Hooker's line a short distance in his front; a brigade or two of the Johnnies got into that ravine and stopped, afraid to go forward, and afraid to go back. Hooker sent an aid to the artillery in our rear with orders to fire down that ravine, and as their position was such they could rake it from end to end, you may imagine the havoc they made; when they cut loose down that hollow, the poor Johnnies were compelled to get out then, and as they ran. Hooker's men let into them with their muskets, and so the racket came to an end.

Some of the prisoners told us they had their scouts out that morning, and as they saw the right of Hooker's line in the air, that is, unprotected, they massed their forces with the intention of going around his flank, and getting in his rear, but they were a little slow in getting there.

When they did come, they ran up against the business end of the 23 Corps, who had got in there, and were fixed for them. This was called the Battle of the Culp Farm; it was reported at the time that there were twenty-one hundred stands of muskets picked up off the field that day.

It was said also that the 14th Kentucky Confederate ran up against the 14th Kentucky Union out there in the woods. Be that as it may, the music was by the full band out there for a few minutes.

Useless for me to say, I forgot all about my headache. It was all knocked out of me for awhile, but it came back on me that night with threefold power, and no sleep did I get. I had to get up and walk about until nearly morning before I got any relief.

Hooker made some complaints in regard to this engagement, and General Sherman scolded him for it; this soured Hooker, and he soon resigned his position, and left our department. Fighting Joe was all right, when there was any fighting to be done, but maybe he had some other fads that Sherman had no use for.

I call to mind that on one occasion the Third Brigade had been resting in the rear for a day or two out of the sounds of the muskets, and it had been quite a relief to us, but now came an order for us to go out and hunt for the rebels, as they were supposed not to be far off.

Company "K" was deployed in front as skirmishers, the balance of the regiment being in rear as supports. We moved along slowly, eyeing every stump, bush or tree for the usual puff of smoke from some hidden foe's musket, but all remained quiet until we struck a cornfield on a hill-side. The corn was about knee high, and we had advanced about half way up the hill towards a public road, when the familiar crack of a carbine came to our ears, and a puff of smoke arose from the corner of a piece of woods on our left, and lazily drifted away.

Two or three of our boys fired at the smoke, but saw nothing. We advanced up to the road, and found a high rail fence on each side of the road, and looking over across an old deadening in close musket range, we saw the enemy's skirmish pits, and they were there ready for business, as the balls that struck those fences bore ample testimony.

We had been sent out to hunt rebels, but as the balls began to whistle around us, and strike those fences, I began to feel as though I had not lost any that I was particular about locating just then.

However, as other skirmishers came up and joined us on the right, we raised a yell, and over those fences we went, and started down through that old deadening.

That Yankee yell was too much for the Johnnies in those skirmish pits; they deserted them at once; their officer, as I suppose, was mounted on a yellow horse, and the way he made "Old Yaller" paw gravel was funny to see; he stood not on the order of going, but went at once.

But while we were having all this fun, the rebs were not idle. As soon as they saw us jump those fences, they opened on us with a jackass battery from their main line half mile away.

Oh! How they did shell us while we were coming down through that deadening. In the hollow, just before we reached the Johnnies' pits, was an old fence row, with a lot of old logs lying in the corners.

A comrade by the name of Reynolds and I were together, and as we were both large men, we were a good target for the shells. As Reynolds and I dropped behind a log in a fence corner, a shell dropped in the corner on the other side, and burst, throwing dirt all over us. It was a splendid shot, and if the fence had not been there, I guess it would have got us both.

We lay there for a few minutes, and then the officer that has charge of us ordered us into the woods on our left. How the Johnnies did yell when they saw us break cover for that woods. They turned their battery on the woods, and while they did us no harm, the racket they made was certainly demoralizing.

There was an old church building in the woods, and some of the officers and men were in there, looking around when a shell came through the building. It is needless to say those men and officers soon sought safer quarters.

With all the shelling, only one man. Corporal David Noble of Co. "K", one of the color guard, was hit on the calf of his leg with a piece of shell, but only disabled him for a few days.

As we had been sent out to find the rebs, and we had located them, our duty for the occasion was performed, and we were ordered to return to camp. As we retraced our steps toward camp, those pesky Johnnies followed us up with that jackass battery, and kept pitching shells at us.

When we got back near camp, we were halted and ordered back out again, but our Lieutenant gave me a gun that he had got somewhere on the raid, and ordered me to take it into camp, and turn it over to the ordinance officer, so I did not get to go back with the boys that afternoon.

There were more troops went out with our brigade on the second trip, and together they cleaned that nest of Johnnies out.

These little noisy skirmishes were of almost daily occurrence on the flanks of the army during this campaign, and while there was a certain amount of danger attached to them at all times, yet we managed to extract a good deal of sport out of them sometimes.

They afforded us very good exercise for our bodies, and kept our sowbelly and hardtack well settled, besides Uncle Sam expected us to be doing something to earn our sixteen dollars per month, and I sincerely believe that I voice the minds of all who were engaged in that campaign, when I say we earned every dollar of it.

STEALING A MARCH ON THE ENEMY

"South of Chattahoochee River, Georgia, July 19th, 1864.

"Dear Parents:—

"Will try to scribble you a few lines today to let you know where I am, and how I am getting along.

"Well, you will see by the heading of this letter that we have crossed the Chattahoochee River, and are now camped within fourteen miles of Atlanta.

"I am not positive, but I think the 23 Corps has the honor of being the first Union troops to cross the river; however, that does not matter. We are on this side; of that I am sure. We crossed at the mouth of Soap Creek on a pontoon bridge; there were a few rebs here guarding this crossing with a twelve pound Howitzer, and were harvesting some wheat near the crossing.

"Our men laid the pontoons in Soap Creek so quietly that the rebs knew nothing about it till they pushed them out of the creek, and across the river, and were popping away at them. The rebs fired their twelve pounder three times, and then our boys captured it. This is what I heard; I did not see it. I give it to you for what it is worth. As usual with us, we are in the woods and bushes, and can't see what's going on only in our own company and brigade.

"Our forces are feeding the wheat to the horses and mules. I would think it made rich feed.

"We have been resting for a few days, but look for a forward movement soon. I suppose the rebs will try hard to hold Atlanta, but they will have to watch General Sherman pretty close, as he seems to be pretty good on flank movements.

"Sherman tried to cut their army in two at Kennesaw Mountains, but failed, but when he tried the flank movement, that was successful.

"The rebs have built miles and miles of strong works all the way down from Dalton, but we have succeeded in flanking them so far; don't know how about it from now on, but I hope for the best.

"I must tell you I have been in some pretty close places since I got down in Georgia. Sometimes I was very uncertain whether I would get out with a whole skin or not, but so far, I have not received a scratch. I cannot say what the future has in store for me, but I trust the Lord will preserve my life in the future from whatever dangers I may be exposed to, as I have faith he has in the past.

"My faith is strong that I will return to my Old Kentucky Home, sound in body and mind, but God's will, not mine, be done.

"Lieutenant Pine came up to us yesterday from Knoxville. He is well and ready to take part in the campaign before us. Will write you again in a few days. This leaves me in good health and spirits. May it hasten to those who wait for tidings from their soldier son."

I am sorry that I did not keep a journal of this Atlanta campaign that I might have followed it, step by step in regular order; then what I might have written would have proven more interesting to the general reader, or even had I written years ago, while the events were fresh in my memory, it would have been better; but to undertake to relate events from memory that happened forty years ago is no easy task.

A great many things that I saw and heard at that time that would have made interesting reading are gone from my memory. I can only remember those things which made deep and lasting impressions on my mind at the time.

I recall to mind one rainy day that the Third Brigade was advancing through a woods, driving the rebel skirmishers ahead of us, the leaden messengers sung around our heads pretty vicious, and we were rushing matters pretty lively, I came to a leaning tree across my path; it was too high from the ground to jump over, and it required a man to stoop pretty low to pass under it, but I was in too much of a hurry to go around it, so I stooped to go under it, and my knapsack caught, and held me.

My first thought was to let my knapsack go, and I began to unbuckle it, when a second thought struck me pretty hard and that was if I lived till night, I would want a dry blanket to wrap up in; so I loosened it from the tree, buckled it on tight, and hastened ahead to regain my place in line. We pushed the rebs back quite a distance that day, and finally came within a few hundred yards of a fort on their main line, and put up breastworks.

By that time it was dark, and I wrapped up in that dry blanket, lay down in the trench, and slept as sweetly as though I had been home on a feather bed, and oh! how thankful I was that I had refrained from throwing away my knapsack.

I was never tempted to do the like again. The next day the rebels evacuated the works in our front, and we took possession.

Our lines here were in the woods as usual; but in the rear of the rebel fort was some cleared land, and a public road ran near the fort back into the country.

Our brigade advanced out this road a short distance and then returned to the fort, and we all lay down to rest. After everything became quiet, I heard a horseman approach the pickets, and heard the pickets challenge him; he told them he was a courier, bringing dispatches to General—, that had had command of the forces in the fort; now the pickets could have captured him very easy had they kept cool and not got excited, but instead of trying to make a prisoner of him, they began to fire at him.

With that he wheeled his horse, and went out that road on the jump as far as I could hear him; it was a pity the boys let him get away, not only for their own sakes, but his dispatches might have been very important to us. Of course, he did not know the Yankees had the fort. He supposed the Confederates still had possession.

It would have proven quite a feather in the boys' caps had they captured him, but they let their nervousness get away with them; they came very near shooting one of their own number; they put a musket ball through his blouse tail. That was a close call.

One night shortly after we came to the front, and the boys were lying in the trenches, trying to get a little sleep, the pickets out in front got to firing pretty rapidly. Finally the firing got so fast and furious that it roused the men in the trenches, and some of them before they got fairly awake, jumped up and began firing also, thinking no doubt from the excitement, that the rebs were right on them.

Vincent Brislear, of Co. "K", the Italian, was one of them that fired, and turning round, he says, "Boys, I gave them one pop; if you all do that well, we will soon have them repulsed". This was fun for the balance of the boys.

Poor Polly Kootchee, as the boys nicknamed him, they plagued him about that pop as long as he remained with us.

There were quite a number of shots fired from the trenches in the excitement, and our boys on picket said the skirmish line was a pretty hot place for a while. Rebs popping away on one side and Yanks on the other.

For a short time, they said they did not know which side of the trees was safest. I was on duty at brigade headquarters that night, and missed the fun. My duty was to awaken the General in case of an alarm, and I of course, performed that duty, but the alarm gradually died away. It was a case of high strung nerves on both sides.

Speaking of nervousness, reminds me of Captain—, who on one occasion had charge of the skirmishers in front of our regiment, during one of our flanking movements.

The skirmishers had advanced to the top of a ridge, and halted behind trees. A short distance in their front were a lot of buildings, around which the rebs were posted, and they and our skirmishers were slinging lead at each other in a way that showed that both were in earnest, and meant business.

Our regiment had halted just under the bridge back of the skirmishers in good supporting distance and laid down. Captain— got terribly excited, and kept calling to Colonel Elsner to bring the regiment up and support him. Colonel Elsner seeing the Captain was nervous, says, "Captain, you are all right, keep cool. I know my business; we are supporting you; it's not our place up there where you are just yet." About this time, one of the Captain's men received a flesh wound across his back, and I don't think I ever heard a man yell louder than he did. This set the Captain's nerves all on edge, and he exclaimed, "There Colonel, one of my men's got his whole back shot off, just because you did not support me." I don't think there was a man in the regiment that understood the matter but took a good laugh over it; even Colonel Elsner's face wore a broad grin.

It was just after this laughable incident that a major of some Kentucky Regiment that had command of the entire detail of skirmishers on this part of the line, came up, and in a ringing voice, ordered the skirmishers forward, and forward they went with a will, and drove the rebs from the buildings, and some distance beyond them.

Then the supports moved up onto the ridge, and as usual put up a line of breastworks. Had we moved up there when that nervous Captain wanted us to, no doubt there would have been several of us killed, as we would have been good targets for those rebs behind the buildings.

The skirmishers could, of course, protect themselves behind trees and stumps, but a line of men in two ranks would have had no protection, so I am glad that we had an officer that did understand his business at that time.

Colonel Elsner was a brave and careful officer. He studied the lay of the ground over which we had to move the regiment, when it was possible that he might protect the lives of his boys, as he called us, and I feel he was right, and deserved credit for it.

General Sherman and General Johnson [sic] were well matched. They watched each other's movements as close as two men playing chess, and while Johnson was gradually compelled to move backwards, he did it so carefully that he rarely gave Sherman any chance to take advantage of his movements.

The Confederate commander was Joseph E. Johnston.—Ed. 2017

Sherman made a mistake when he tried to cut through Johnson's lines at Kennesaw Mountains, at least it proved to be a failure; the movement was all right had it proven a success. Sherman's idea was to cut Johnson's army into; had he succeeded in doing so, it would have been a crushing blow to Johnson, but the fortifications on and around Kennesaw were too strong for an assault of that kind.

Sherman lost many brave men there, whose lives might have been saved had he done at first what he was compelled to do later—resume his flanking movements.

Our position the day of the assault was on the right flank of the army, but we could hear the thunder of the guns.

"In the trenches in front of Atlanta, Ga. July 25th, 1864.

"My Dear Parents:—

"There have been lively times down here since I wrote you my letter of the 19th.

"Since the rebel army fell back across the Chattahoochee River, General Johnson, their commander has been relieved and General [John Bell] Hood has taken command. He seems to be a fighter from away back, though a somewhat reckless one.

"After our corps left our camps at the river, we marched to Decatur, a small town five miles from Atlanta in the direction of Stone Mountain. It took us nearly three days as we had to fight the rebel cavalry all the way. They tried hard to keep us back, but failed to do so. At the same time, the 15th Corps was still farther to our left, and tore up the railroad from Stone Mountain to Decatur.

"The 16th and 17th Corps came up in our rear, and we moved to the right, and took position in the center, the 4th, 14th and 20th Corps being on our right.

"We found the enemy entrenched in our front, but on the morning of the 22nd, we found the trenches empty, and at daylight, we moved up and invested their main line in front of Atlanta.

"In the meantime the new commander of the enemy had not been idle. During the night of the 21st and the morning of the 22nd, he had massed his forces on the left and rear of the 15th, 16th and 17th Corps, and about the middle of the day jumped on them with both feet.

"For once the boys in grey had managed to surprise the boys in blue, but only for a short time; our boys soon got straightened out, and a terrible battle was fought; part of it in the open fields and woods, and part behind breastworks. Our men in the works would repulse a charge in front, and then jump over the works and face, the rear, and repulse a charge from that direction.

"The battle lasted till night shut down, leaving the boys in blue masters of the field; the loss on both sides was heavy. On our side, we suffered the loss of the gallant McPherson, a brave and noble officer. He will be sadly missed by the brave boys he commanded, who all loved him.

"Thomas Sherin of Company "K" was struck in the breast with a shell or solid shot that day, and killed. The same shot struck Henry C. Hall of Company "K", and cut off one of his legs below the knee.

"Labon Winchester, a North Carolinian, who enlisted in Company "K", while we were at Knoxville, Tennessee, was also wounded while on the skirmish line. It is doubtful if Hall and he get well. So you see they will pick on Company 'K' once in awhile.

"There was heavy cannonading last night, and this morning on our right. Guess Old Fighting Joe is having a game of ball with the Johnnies.

"We are in position about one mile from the City of Atlanta. Between us and the city the rebs have a strong line of fortifications. I think Uncle Billy [Sherman] will have to do some more flanking before we get Atlanta.

"Our batteries amuse themselves by pitching shells into town at intervals. I don't think I want to be a resident of the town at present. I fear it is not very healthy.

"[Union cavalry general, Judson] Killpatrick and Stoneman are raiding around, trying to cut the rebels' haversack strings. I wish them success.

"Now I have written you quite a lengthy letter for me, so will close for this time. I am still in fine health, and wish you all the same blessing."

On the morning of the 22nd of July, we found the rebel works in our front empty, the enemy having moved out of them in the night. We at once moved forward, and took position in front of the Howard house.

We formed our line at the edge of the timber that surrounded the Howard house. If I remember rightly, it was pasture land in our front, gradually sloping down to a ravine, and then gently ascending upward till it reached the top of a ridge, on which the rebels had built a strong line of fortifications just outside of the city of 'Atlanta.

The distance from our line to the rebel line was perhaps four or five hundred yards, but this is only guess work; it might not have been near that, for I know we could see the works very plainly.

We had not been there long till we began to hear firing away to our left and front. It kept rolling nearer an nearer, increasing in volume till the very earth shook with the thunder of artillery and the rattle of musketry, and it kept moving around our left flank until it seemed to be almost in our rear.

Us fellows in the center, not knowing the condition to our left, began to feel pretty shaky, for we did not know how to account for that firing in our rear, unless the rebels were driving our men back.

But after awhile, the firing began to work more on a line with us, and then we felt better. I could have seen part of the battlefield by going about a hundred yards to our left, but dared not leave my place on the line, for we did not know what minute we would be called into action, but everything remained quiet in our front.

General Sherman's headquarters were at the Howard House, just in our rear during the battle, and it was there they took the body of the brave McPherson after he was killed.

Sherman was actually occupying the Augustus Hurt House, which was erroneously listed as the Howard House in official documents. Today, a marker for the house stands in the parking lot of the Carter Presidential Center.—Ed. 2017

Thus we missed another big battle, not by being on the flank this time, but by being in the center. There had been a battle a few days before this, if I am not mistaken, that we missed then, if I remember rightly.

There was another battle July 28th on our right; that we missed also; it appeared to be our luck to be left out, but I don't call to mind now that I heard the boys make any complaints about it.

Shortly after we had taken our position that morning near the Howard House, a detail was called for from Company "K" to help throw up an earthwork for a battery somewhere on our left, I think.

The men detailed were Henry C. Hall and Peter Albeats. Comrade Thomas Sherin of Company "K" spoke up, and said, "'Pete, give me a chew of tobacco, and I will go in your place.". "All right," said Peter, and he cut Tom a piece of tobacco, and gave it to him. Hall and Sherin then went over to the battery, and began work. They had not been at work long until a solid shot or shell from a rebel battery struck Sherin in the breast, and killed him. The same' shot cut off one of Hall's legs, so I may say that comrade Thomas Sherin was killed for a chew of tobacco.

General Hood, knowing and understanding the reasons why his government at Richmond had taken the command of the army away from Johnston, and given it to him, thought he must do something to show that the change was for the better; hence after he took command until after July 28th, he made some quick moves, and did some sharp, stubborn fighting, but finding he was only wasting his army and losing ground, he withdrew behind his entrenchments, and renewed the same old game that Johnson had played, watching for a good opportunity to jump us.

General Sherman in the meantime began to reach out with his army towards the Macon railroad, running south from the city of Atlanta, well knowing that if he could get possession of that road in Hood's rear, that Hood would be compelled to give up Atlanta, as that road was the Confederate cornbread line.

So General Scofield, commander of the 23rd Corps, commenced to move his troops toward the right flank once more.

We had daily skirmishes with the Johnnies, and got into some pretty close places, where they made it hot for us, but we established our lines and held them.

DEATH OF COLONEL ELSNER

"On the Firing Line, near the Macon R. R.

"Southwest of Atlanta, Ga., August 10. 1864.

"My Dear Parents, Brothers and Sisters:

"I am thankful I have another opportunity afforded me of writing to you all, and to acknowledge the receipt of your kind letter of August 1st.

"I was rejoiced to learn you were all well. Glad to tell you also I am enjoying that same blessing, but I must tell you that during the past week we have been in some tough places.

"Our corps has kept swinging around on the right flank until we are not far from the Macon railroad. We skirmished with, us that it required about all the nerve we had to stay with them, but so far we hold all the ground we have taken.

"On August 3rd we took a very commanding position from them, and although they gave us an unmerciful shelling, we had taken ahold, and like bulldogs we held on, and fortified the position to suit ourselves.

"August 8th the Fiftieth were all on the skirmish line, and pushed the rebs back about two miles. Colonel Elsner gallantly leading the regiment, but in the last charge we made, where the Colonel wanted to drive the enemy from some buildings, we had just started with a yell, when the brave Colonel fell, shot in the head by a minie ball.

"He died instantly, but we went on, and drove the enemy from those buildings, and away beyond them.

"The command of the regiment now fell on Major Galespie. I don't think there was hardly a man in the regiment but what shed tears when they learned that Colonel Elsner was killed, for we all loved him, but that kind voice is hushed in death; we will never hear it pleading with us again to be good boys, as we have in the past. Lieutenant Reed of Company 'I' went to Cincinnati yesterday with his remains. May they rest in peace.

"Joseph Carson of Company 'K' was wounded in the hand this morning by a minie ball, while we were eating breakfast in the trenches. I was seated in front of him at the time, and my head was near catching the same ball; his wound is slight; he will be all right in a few days. This is the third time he has been wounded since entering the service. At Perryville, Ky., a musket ball entered his breast and came out his back. He is both unlucky and lucky.

"Our rifle pits where we are now are not over two hundred yards from the rebel rifle pits. We are so close we have to change the pickets after night; our brigade has just finished the thirty-third line of breastworks since we came to the front.

"I am getting tired of this unceasing pop, pop, popping of the pickets, and boom, boom, boom of the artillery, and the crash of the bursting shells. It's the same thing over every day. When and how will it end? is a question we often ask ourselves. Ah, well! all good and bad things must end sometime. We are sure we are in the right, and we know the right will conquer in the end, and the end must come sooner or later.

"The day that Colonel Elsner was killed, the 8th day of August, I was 21 years of age. It was rather a sad birthday for me—but such is life.

"The order has just been given for Company 'K' to get ready for the picket line tonight, so I will finish this tomorrow if my life is spared, so I bid you good-night?"

"August 11th, 1864.

"I am glad to have it to say this morning that Company 'K' all got back off the skirmish line safe and sound. Everything seems to be quiet along the lines this morning.

"It is whispered among the knowing ones that General Sherman is going to try a grand flanking movement, and that troops are already passing our rear towards our right flank. If that be true, look out for startling news from this point before many days.

"We draw pretty good rations now, and have plenty to eat. It is well that we do, for our work is so hard we could not keep up otherwise.

"I have just learned that Lieutenant Reed will not go any farther than Marietta, Ga., with the Colonel's body, but that Elsner's brother will meet him there and take the body to Cincinnati.

"The mail is going out, so I will close for this time. Will write again in a few days. My love and best wishes to all."

"Near Macon R. R., Southwest of Atlanta, Ga,.

"August 22nd, 1864.

"'Dear Parents:

"Well, we are still in the same position on the line that we were when I wrote you last.

"The Confederate General Hardee's troops are in our front; his pickets and our brigade pickets have compromised, and will not fire on each other without warning; they are not much over one hundred yards apart. Their butternut clothes are so much the color of dead leaves, it is hard to detect them. Since the compromise, it has been very quiet in our front. Each party gets out front of their pits, and talk to each other a little.

"The rebel officers will not allow their men to hold very long chats with our boys. A rebel Sergeant came over, and gave himself up last night. He reports their lines much weakened in places, as they have had to stretch them out so long to keep us from cutting their railroad.

"He says if we get possession of the road once, their army would have to leave here in double-quick, as that would shut off their supplies.

"I understand the enemy's cavalry have cut our road between here and Dalton, but it will not amount to much, as they can't hold it long enough to do us any harm.

"Killpatrick, on our side, has been trying to cut the Macon road, but so far it has not amounted to anything.

"The firing of the pickets was very annoying when we first took positions on this part of the line; the balls would come whistling over our heads pretty vicious; sometimes they would hit the tree-tops, and then glance down among us.

"The other day Lieutenant Pine was sitting in his tent, doing some writing, when a ball struck a tree over him, glanced down and thumped him on the head. It did him no harm, as it was just about spent when it struck him, and only drew a few drops of blood.

"The same day, I think it was, a ball came over the works, passed through three or four tents and struck Comrade Shepard on the breast. We all thought the way he yelled the ball had gone through him. We ran to him, and he was holding his hand on his breast, and still kept yelling. We got him to take his hand down and the flattened bullet dropped to the ground. It had not even penetrated his clothes.

"When he found out he was still alive, he began to curse the rebels, both loud and deep, and I can assure you he called them anything but gentlemen. I never heard a man curse harder. Why, Company 'K' quarters were blue with smoke and smelled of brimstone for an hour afterward.

"Shepard is from North Carolina, and enlisted in Company 'K' while we were at Knoxville. He has a black and blue lump on his breast the size of a hen's egg, where the ball struck him.

"We got the first mail this morning that we have received for seven days, but no letters came for me. I trust I will be more lucky next time.

"Well, according to the books, I have been in the service two years today. I have one more year to serve, and then if God spares my life, I will come home. A year will soon pass away.

"There is some movement going on in our rear, and the wise ones say Sherman has a trump card up his sleeve that he intends playing before long. I am satisfied myself that there is trouble brewing for someone, so you can listen for something to drop with a dull thud in this part of Georgia before long.

"I close for this time with love and good wishes for you all."

The 8th of August was a sad day for the Fiftieth boys. A regiment was called for to drive the rebels from our front. A Kentucky regiment from our brigade had fallen into line and started, when Acting Brigadier General Strickland called them back, and said he wanted his regiment, the Fiftieth Ohio to go out. As I was not feeling well. Lieutenant Pine told me to remain in camp, and I did so. What took place that afternoon, I am not able to relate, only as the boys told me.

They had driven the rebs back quite a distance, and as the shades of night began to settle down over the scene, the rebs had made a stand around some farm buildings.

Colonel Elsner told the boys he wished to drive them from those buildings, and then they would stop.

As I understand, he had just given the order forward, when he received the fatal shot. The boys drove the rebs from those buildings, and followed them into the woods beyond.

In the meantime, darkness had settled down, and our boys and the rebs got mixed together. The rebel officers were giving our officers commands what to do in order to bag the Yankees, thinking they were talking to their own officers. As luck would have it, our officers saw and understood the situation, and gave the order on the quiet for the Fiftieth to move by the left flank, and escape the trap.

A few minutes more, and they would likely have all been taken prisoners. They were lucky to escape.

The Fiftieth Ohio were a sad looking lot of boys next morning. In losing Colonel Elsner, we all felt we had lost a kind friend, and a brave and trustful officer.

His remains were sent home to Ohio, and laid to rest in beautiful Spring Grove. It is sad to think that one before whom perhaps a brilliant future was unfolding should have his life snuffed out in a moment, but his was only one among thousands that met this fate during this cruel war.

His death added one more to that mighty host who freely gave their lives for the honor of that old flag they loved so well, and thank God, they did not die in vain, for today that flag is honored by all the civilized nations of the world.

This place on the line southwest of Atlanta that we now held, we were placed in very quietly one evening after dark, and ordered to put up breastworks, but to be careful and not make any noise, as we were very near the rebel lines.

I was ordered to station myself a few paces in front of the Company to give warning in case of danger. The boys worked very quietly and by daylight had a very good trench dug. Only one shot was fired in our front during the night, and that was fired while I was on guard. I suppose some Johnnie got suspicious that something was doing over in our direction, but no one replied to his shot and his bullet did not find a Yankee but it passed not far from where I stood.

When daylight came, the rebs were surprised to see the blue-coats so near them behind a good line of rifle pits.

Our line was in the edge of the timber, a small field in our front sloping down to a ravine and on the next rise in the edge of the timber were the rebel rifle pits; the two lines were not over two hundred yards apart, and now each party made it hot for the other for a few days.

This proved to be the last line of works we were to occupy hear Atlanta, while the rebels held the city.

The 23rd Corps were the last troops to withdraw from this line when Sherman swung his army onto the Macon railroad. Company "K" was on the picket line the last day we were there, but everything was quiet, as we had compromised with the Johnnies in our front.

We were taking it easy, sitting outside our pits sunning ourselves; the 4th Corps had withdrawn from our left, and their works were empty, and some sharp-eyed Johnnie in nosing around, found this out, and advanced and got into one of the empty pits. Glancing over our way and seeing us all sitting outside our pits like birds, he could not resist the temptation of trying a shot at us. Lucky for us, his aim was bad, but presto! change! in one minute's time not a Yank could be seen, the way we disappeared in our holds would have put a colony of prairie dogs to shame.

It is likely some of us returned him a compliment at the time, but I have no remembrance of it. We quietly withdrew from the line that night, and followed the balance of the army towards the Macon railroad.

I recall to mind that Company "K" was on the skirmish line one day while we held this position, and we had orders to keep up a hot fire on the rebs' position all day to draw their attention to us, while some movement took place on another part of the line.

Well, we certainly obeyed orders to the letter. The pickets would commence away on our right to fire one at a time, until it would run the length of the brigade. Then we would all yell, and the right would commence and fire by squads until it would reach our left. And thus we kept it up all day.

It was rare sport for us, and I suppose the rebs wondered what it all meant. Well, they were put wise a few days later.

"25 miles South of Atlanta, Ga.,

"Near Lovejoy Station, September 4th, 1864.

"Dear Parents, Brothers and Sisters:

"I believe I wrote you not long ago that General Sherman had a trump card up his sleeve. Well, he has played it, and it proved to be the joker, and won for us all the city of Atlanta.

"General Sherman placed the 20th Corps at the crossing of the Chattahoochee River and then swung the balance of the army on to the Macon R. R.

"The movement completely surprised General Hood. He knew there was a movement going on, but he seemed to think that Sherman was falling back. He telegraphed to Richmond that the Yankees were in full retreat towards the bogs of Dalton, and he and his officers were having a ball in Atlanta the night of September 1st, when a courier hastily approached and informed him that Sherman had possession of his cornbread line. Sherman had a part of the rebel army on the railroad, driving them ahead of him. The 23rd Corps, as usual, was guarding the left flank of the army, and missed the hard fighting. But the Army of the Tennessee had some pretty stiff fighting to do, but all the same they drove the enemy before them till night coming on put a stop to the fighting.

"In the meantime Hood evacuated Atlanta, burning up several carloads of fixed ammunition, and blowing up quite a number of magazines.

"We could hear the noise of the bursting shells, and it sounded like a big battle going on. Hood, with the troops left in Atlanta, took a road that led around farther to our left, and went around us and succeeded in forming a junction with the remnant of his army in our front, and thus we have them all before us once more.

"As soon as the 20th Corps at the river learned that Hood had left Atlanta they moved up and took possession. I believe that we will fall back to Atlanta now and rest, as we only came out here with twelve days' rations to do us twenty, so I judge we will fall back nearer our base of supplies.

"I hope we will go back to Atlanta, as I have a curiosity to see the place that we besieged so long.

"We got plenty of green corn and sweet potatoes on our way here, so we did fine on our rations.

"It appears as though we always get shelled on the 3rd of the month. On the 3rd of July we got shelled, and on the 3rd of August we got shelled, and yesterday, the 3rd of September, we got shelled, but no one got hurt in our regiment yesterday.

"Our brigade now consists of the 123rd and 91st Indiana, 20th and 27th Kentucky, and the 50th Ohio. It is claimed that we have built forty lines of entrenchments since we came to the front.

"This is Sunday, and we are all taking a much-needed rest; the sun is shining very warm and pleasant; the days are warm, but the nights are cool. Will write you again in a few days. This leaves me in good health and spirits. Trusting it may find you all enjoying the same, I close for. this time."

"Decatur, Ga., September 21st, 1864.

"Our corps has fallen back to this place, which is six miles east of Atlanta.

"We are strongly entrenched, and ready for the Johnnies if they wish to call on us. We have all been up to Atlanta, and must say we found it a pretty badly used-up town. It is safe to say hardly a house in the place has escaped being hit by shells or bullets; the depot is completely riddled. What few citizens remained in town had holes dug in the ground for refuge, when the batteries would be throwing shells into the town.

"Now, as to Hood's night retreat from Atlanta, it must have been a hasty one.

"We marched over part of their line of retreat as we came from Lovejoy here, and all along the route they had thrown away anything and everything that would impede their progress: bake-ovens, cornmeal, stretchers, wagons and ambulances were scattered all along the road that they marched over. It looks as though they almost fell over one another in their haste to get away.

"We passed several field hospitals coming from Lovejoy or Jonesborough here, and there we could see the horrors of war—men lying in the woods and fields all around Jonesborough, where the fighting was done; some dead, some dying, some with their arms and legs cut off, and lying by their sides; here you could see three or four fingers, and there three or four toes, that had been cut off by the doctor and flung aside. It looked hard, but such is war.

"All the enemy's dead and wounded fell into the hands of our troops, who are caring for them as fast as they can.

"We are having a very good time here. It is certainly a relief to us to be out of hearing of the whistling of bullets and the crashing of bursting shells. Picket duty here is very light.

"Our duty from day to day is brigade, battalion, company and squad drill. We are playing soldiers again now, but coming down through Georgia we saw soldiering in reality. The paymaster made us a visit the other day and paid us six months' pay. We appreciated his visit very much.

"Now, I must close, so, dear parents, be of good cheer—the world goes well with me, and may its cares rest lightly upon you all, is my best wish and prayer."

While at Jonesborough, on the line one evening, our brass band came up near the breastworks and were giving us some very good music. They had candles lit so they could see their music, and we were all enjoying the concert very much, but the rebs did not enjoy it so well, and they pitched a shell or two at the light, and that ended the concert.

The rebs were mad anyhow, and did not feel like listening to Yankee music.

HOOD TRIES TO CUT OUR HAVERSACK STRINGS

"Decatur, Ga., September 28th, 1864.

"Dear Parents:

"Your kind letter received a few days ago reminds me of my duty of writing to you and acknowledging my negligence. With duty pressing me, I am too apt to forget that you may feel anxious about me, but rest assured that I never cease in my affection nor forget for a moment how much I am indebted to the best of parents.

"I am happy to tell you I am in the best of health at this time. We all feel proud for what has been accomplished since the 1st of May—not only in our own department, but also in the others.

"Grant on the Weldon Railroad, [Union Admiral David] Farragut at Mobile, and [General Philip] Sheridan and Averill in the Shenandoah Valley—all these splendid victories are enough to rejoice the hearts of all who love the old flag, and especially those who are fighting to keep it from being trailed in the dust.

"Yes, we feel very much encouraged and think that another year will see the close of the war. The Confederates are losing ground everywhere, and sooner or later they will be compelled to lay down their arms, and then victory will perch on the banner of the Union.

"I enclose in this letter General Sherman's official details of the capture of Atlanta. I think it will interest you.

"I have no idea how long we will remain here; it is hard to tell what the next move will be. Everything appears to be very quiet at present, but it would not take long for either side to kick up a rumpus, if they would decide to do so. And it may be that Sherman or Hood, one or the other, will start the ball rolling again before long.

"Decatur has been a nice little place. I say 'has been,' for now it shows it has had rough treatment. Soldiers have been around and through it so much, it is pretty badly battered up, the same as Atlanta. It seems like a shame to see so much property destroyed, but such is war.

"The country that the armies have marched and fought over will show the effects of it for years after the war is over."

While camped at Decatur, the Fiftieth Ohio was detailed to go out with some wagons one day after forage. We went out in the direction of Stone Mountain. I do not remember if there were any other troops with us or not, except a few cavalrymen for advance and rear guards. We got our forage all right, and the boys as well as the wagons were all loaded down.

We found plenty of sweet potatoes, and someone in my squad found a hog running loose and confiscated it. I had one of the hams on my bayonet, and my haversack full of sweet potatoes. Everything passed off nicely until we started back toward the camp. Not a reb had shown themselves all day, and naturally our boys got a little careless.

In going out in the morning, we had passed a good well of water in the corner of a piece of woods, close beside the road, and nearby on the same side of the road was a house. We noticed no one at the house as we went out, but when we came back, there were four or five young ladies in the yard. The Fiftieth Ohio had just got a new flag, and those ladies went into ecstasy over that new flag. They said it was the prettiest thing they ever saw in their lives.

They seemingly did their best to get some of the boys or officers to stop in, but as good luck would have it, none of them halted, though I must admit the ladies looked charming.

We all passed on to the well, and quite a number of the boys stopped to get water. Our squad of cavalry rear guards closed up and stopped also.

Just about this time, a squad of rebel cavalry from somewhere charged into the boys at the well, and also into our rear, took a few prisoners, and I think, wounded a man or two, as a good many shots were fired on both sides, and then the Johnnies dashed away again.

The road was narrow after passing the well, and was lined on either side with heavy pine underbrush, and all we could do when the firing commenced, was to form a line of battle along the road.

I had my ham on my bayonet, and I did not know what to do, but concluded I would hang to it for awhile, until I saw how matters went. Fortunately, I was permitted to get it into camp safely.

The rebs followed us for quite a distance, and made two or three more dashes at our rear, but our cavalry guards did not permit them to reach the infantry boys anymore; and what prisoners they took at first, I think all got away by dodging into the thickets.

Now, I believe those young ladies knew what was going to happen, and were trying to decoy some of the officers or men into that house to have them captured. It was lucky none of them went in, for if they had, they would have been very likely to have taken a trip to Andersonville [Prison].

I will just add there was no more straggling done that night after the rebs made their first dash.

I remember one day while we were on the Atlanta Campaign that a comrade was shot out on the skirmish line, and a squad volunteered to go out, and bring in the body.

Comrade Caldwell took the hospital flag, and went with them. The body lay in a clear space in the woods in full view and close rifle range of the rebel skirmishers.

Caldwell waved his flag, but the rebs would not respect it, but instead sent a perfect storm of lead that direction; another of the squad fell mortally wounded, and they picked him up instead of the dead comrade, and ran in with him.

In the meantime, Comrade Caldwell remained at his post, waving his flag, even after the other comrades had left him, while the balls were kicking up the leaves all around him. He had to be called before he would leave his position; this shows he had grit, as well as the comrade he describes in his verses.

Now, kind reader, go back to Decatur, where you left me with a haversack full of sweet potatoes, and a ham of fresh meat on my bayonet.

When we got into camp that night, we received the news that General Hood had played a joke on us; he was on our railroad in our rear, cutting up high jinx. Next morning, October 4th, we broke camp, and started after him.

"Yalesville, Alabama, October 22nd, 1864.

"Sherman's army is all here except the 20th Corps, which is holding on to Atlanta. We have been on the move almost daily since the 4th of October.

"No general engagement has taken place, but there have been several small scraps by different detachments.

"I suppose you have learned ere this that General Hood moved his army to our rear and tore up the railroad in different places, but as he doesn't appear able to hold it, I don't see as it will do us very much harm.

"I have no time to write any particulars, as the mail leaves in a few minutes. Wish Hood had remained quiet a while longer. We were situated very comfortably at Decatur, but I suppose the harder the storm the sooner it will be over. Hope to let you hear from me again soon."

"Cedar Bluff, Alabama, October 27, 1864.

"Am still on the land, and among the living, and in the best of health.

"The 23rd Corps has been dodging around quite lively since leaving Decatur, but have not been able to see many rebs; only a few dead ones at Allatoona Pass, where General Corse had a fight with them, and held his ground, thereby saving a large amount of commissary stores for the use of Sherman's army.

"Then we saw also a few prisoners down at Rome that our cavalry Captured. I am not able to say just where General Hood's army is, but it is down in here somewhere. Don't know whether General Sherman will be able to bring him to bay or not.

"I will name some of the most important places we have passed through, since we have been on this march: Decatur, Atlanta, Marietta, Acworth, Allatoona, Cartersville, Cass Station, Cassville, Kingston, Rome, Calhoun, Resaca, Villanow, Somerville, Melville, Georgia; Yalesville, Alabama, and thence to Cedar Bluff, where we are at the present time. We have been resting for a few days.

"I can give you no idea when we will move, or where we will go when we do move. We had fine weather for marching; it is getting stormy now, but still remains warm, but stormy weather is not very agreeable to soldiers in the field.

"We are guarding a pontoon bridge at present over the Coosa River. A rumor is circulating in camp that Colonel Strickland is to be placed in command at Lexington, Ky., but as it came in over the grapevine '*Telaliegraph*' of course it is a fake.

"I believe I have told you all that would interest you this time, so will close for the present."

"Chattanooga, Tennessee, November 5th, 1864."

"Well, we are back in Tennessee once more. When I wrote you last we were in Cedar Bluff, Alabama, but we left there in great haste and came here. Our brigade had to guard the wagon train through, while the balance of the Corps came through by rail.

"We are resting, and drawing clothing and rations today.

"It is claimed we have marched four hundred and twenty miles since leaving Decatur a month ago; that would be an average of fourteen miles a day, but there were several days we rested by the way. Those who are supposed to know say we are going somewhere to the left of Nashville to meet General Hood, as he is down in there with his army threatening Nashville. I don't think any of his army will see Nashville, except as prisoners of war.

"Well, three more days, and we are going to elect 'Uncle Abe' for four years more. I am going to give him my vote, and best wishes.

"We came through some very pretty country on the way here. I stood the marching first-rate. When they came to stack arms at night, I was always in my place. I am proud to say I have never given my officers the opportunity of calling me a straggler since I came into the service; never missed but twice being on the firing line with them in the Atlanta Campaign, and then I was lawfully excused by my commanding officer.

"Will try to come home, the Lord willing, with a clean record. Will write you again in a few days, if I am permitted the opportunity."

"Chattanooga, November 6th, 1864."

"We are still lying here in camp this morning. Would love to take a trip onto Lookout Mountain and Missionary Ridge, but as we don't know what minute we will be called on to move, I dare not leave camp.

"Lookout Mountain is where 'Fighting Joe' fought the rebs above the clouds. The rebs had a strong position on Lookout Mountain and Missionary Ridge; it hardly looks possible that they could have been driven away so easily, but the boys in blue got them just the same. But here is Billy calling for the mail, so I must say good-bye for this time."

While General Corse was fighting the battle of Allatoona Pass we were on our way there, and could hear the guns, but when we arrived there the battle was over. We saw a good many dead Johnnies lying on the field, where they fell.

General Sherman sent that celebrated dispatch from Pine Mountain to General Corse to hold the fort over our heads, as we were marching along in the valley between the two.

While we were at Rome, our second division was sent out to support the cavalry one morning. We went out, I think in the direction of what is called the Smoky Mountains. The cavalry soon ran into a force of the Johnnies camped in the woods, and routed them before they had their breakfast cooked and eaten.

The rebs had two pieces of artillery with them, which they put in position on a small ridge in the road, and began to fire on the cavalry. On either side of the road, where the artillery was posted, was a ravine running parallel with the road, which was well hidden by the thick underbrush that grew on the bank.

Some of the cavalry, as I was told, dismounted, and flanked up those ravines, while a heavy force made a strong demonstration on the road in front; this movement in front drew the attention of the rebs, and they never saw the flankers till they rushed for the guns, and captured them.

Word came back to us infantry that the guns were captured, but we thought the news too good to be true, but we soon came to where the guns had been limbered up, and were standing in a field with the rebel drivers sitting on their horses. As I understood, they wished to drive into Rome.

Some of our boys in passing made the remark that the Johnnies looked pretty hard; the Johnnies overheard them, and replied, "You would look hard too, if you had been on the go as we have the last month."

The cavalry did not need any supporting that day; they kept up a running fight with the Johnnies, and ran them out into the Smoky Mountains. I do not remember whether there was any loss on our side or not, but it is quite likely there was. I remember seeing several dead Johnnies along the road.

We started on our return shortly after noon. Before crossing the river into Rome, we had quite a long hill to descend, and quite a stretch of bottom to cross. The 50th Ohio Regiment was pretty well in the rear, so I got a good view of nearly all the second division on the move.

The magnificent spectacle they presented to my sight that evening lingers in my memory yet. Each regiment, as they trailed down the long hill, and across the bottom to the river, had their flags unfurled to the breeze, and their bands playing.

The guns of the troops were carried at a right shoulder shift, and they shone in the bright evening sunshine like burnished silver. The scene was an inspiring one, and made such an impression on my mind, I have never forgotten it.

I was not the only one to admire it; the citizens of Rome were all out to view it, men women and children; they had heard of the capture of the two guns, and were very anxious to see if it was true.

The cavalry deserved great credit for their work that day, for they hustled the Johnnies from start to finish.

A NIGHT'S MARCH TO FRANKLIN

"Spring Hill, Tennessee, November 10th, 1864.

"My Dear Parents:

"I seat myself this beautiful, bright morning to let you know my present whereabouts.

The last letter I wrote you I was at Chattanooga. We boarded the cars there the same day I wrote you, and came to Nashville, and from there to this place, which is about twenty-five miles south of Nashville.

"This is as far as we could go by rail at present, as there is a bridge washed away.

"We were glad to get out of the cars. We were on them two days and nights and had gotten very tired of them. It rained all the time we were on board, so our trip here was not a very agreeable one. The weather has cleared up now, and we feel like ourselves once more.

"This is a fine country here; a lovely farming country, from what I can see. It does not seem to be hurt by the war so far.

"I see plenty of fat cattle, hogs, chickens, turkeys, geese and ducks. There ought not to be any danger of starving in a country where eatables are as plentiful as they appear to be here.

"It is a little hard just now to keep trace of the 23rd Corps. I understand the balance of our division is at Johnsonville. I don't know where the Corps headquarters is at present; neither do I know where Sherman's headquarters are, but I judge he is somewhere near Atlanta, Ga.

"It is rumored here that Sherman intends marching the troops he has with him farther south somewhere. I can't say how true it is, but think it quite likely he has some scheme that he wishes to try. I trust he may succeed wherever he goes.

"Well, election day is past, and I cast my first vote for President. I voted for Abraham Lincoln. There were some few in the 50th Ohio that voted for George B. McClellan, but not a great many. I suppose we will know in a few days who has won, but I have not the least doubt but 'Uncle Abe' will draw the prize. I think he is the man that ought to have it. He was in at the beginning of the trouble, and I would like to see him remain until it is ended.

"This makes the fourth letter I have written without receiving an answer, but am looking for a letter now every day.

"I think we will move farther south in a few days, as the 23rd Corps and the 4th Corps has been sent into this State to look after General Hood, so we will be very likely to get down to business in a few days, as I learn Hood is headed this way. This leaves me in good health."

One little incident that happened election day in Company "K" might be worth relating: Comrade Joseph Stagmire, a German, whom I have mentioned once before in these reminiscences, was a McClellan man, and by some means, he managed to get hold of some whiskey, and got pretty full. The boys got to plaguing him about voting for McClellan, and he got very angry. Finally he exclaimed in his broken English, "He who not vote for McClellan been a God for damn sunver bitch." This added fuel to the flames; the boys ran him still higher now, and had their own fun with him. Poor Stagmire! Of course he was ashamed of it when he got sober, but the boys did not let him forget election day very

I am proud to put it on record that I cast my first Presidential vote for that noble patriot, Abraham Lincoln. It is sad to think that the assassin's bullet should have cut him down just when he was about to see his great desire accomplished—the preservation of the Union and the restoration of the Government.

Had the enemies let him live, matters would have been adjusted a great deal better than they were. Poor, martyred President—he died with a broken heart.

"Columbia, Tennessee, November 18th, 1864.

"Dear Parents, Brothers and Sisters:

"It is my pleasant task this delightful morning to seat myself to answer your kind message, which has just come to hand.

"I can assure you I was pleased to hear from you all and learn you were well and doing well. We received our mail this morning, the first for fifteen days.

"We have been on the move so much, it was hard for our mail to catch us; perhaps we will stop here a few days, at least that is what

Colonel Strickland told us when he brought us into this camp, but I do not know that he can tell anything more about it than the rest of us.

"Columbia is a very pretty little town, situated on the south bank of Duck River. There is a large fort here, mounting eighteen guns. The fort is situated so as to command the town and surrounding country. We are camped on a beautiful hill, overlooking the river. There is a large spring near camp, that would supply General Sherman's army, which is a fine thing for us, and we appreciate it very much.

"Well, 'Uncle Abe' was elected all right. George B. will have to wait awhile. Maybe he can get there later. We wanted no change till this trouble is settled. Time enough then for a change.

"General Hood is down here south of us somewhere, not far off. Rumor says he is headed this way, so we may have a visit from him before long. Well, if he comes, we will do the best w-e can. I hardly think we have force enough down here to face him in a general engagement, but I suppose General Scofield knows what he can do. Sherman sent him here to look after Hood, and I presume he will do it.

"I don't know just where any of them are, but they are south of here somewhere.

"The last letter I wrote you, we were in camp at Spring Hill, eleven miles north of here, but we did not remain there but a few days until we were sent on here.

"Everything is in such an unsettled condition down here at present, it is impossible for me to tell where I may be when I have the opportunity to write you again, but rest assured I will write whenever the opportunity presents itself, and I have anything of importance to write.

"This leaves me in good health, and trusting you all are enjoying the same God's blessing."

Little did I dream when I penned the above lines what the future held in store for me. What a blessing it is that we cannot read our future; if we could, what miserable beings we would be sometimes; but the Father above has so ordered it that men and women may be happy right up to the moment that calamity overtakes them.

Death even often overtakes persons with a smile on their face, yet I have read of quite a number of soldiers that have had a warning or premonition of death before going into battle, but this is the exception, and not the rule.

Had I known at this time what I was to experience in the next five months, I certainly would have written a great deal different from what I did, but I am thankful that the future was a sealed book to me at the time.

General Hood at this time had his army at Florence, Alabama, and General Scofield had his little army at Pulaski, Tennessee, consisting of a part of the 23rd and 4th Corps, and Sherman about this time was leaving Atlanta with his army on his grand march to the sea.

General Hood, on or about the 21st of November, began his march northward, and by a flank movement compelled General Scofield to fall back to Columbia, reaching the latter place November 24th, barely in time, General Cox says in his book, to keep General Hood from heading him off.

We remained in our position at Columbia until the 24th, when the enemy's movement on our left flank forced us to abandon Columbia and retire to the north side of Duck River.

Strickland's 3rd Brigade was placed in line with the rest of the two divisions to guard the crossings of the river. A large crowd of contrabands crossed the pontoon while we were here, fleeing from Hood's army. I never saw them anymore. I do not know whether they escaped the enemy or not.

Here we remained till the evening of the 29th, the Johnnies in the meantime amusing themselves at intervals by pitching a few shells at us, and quite often a minie ball would come buzzing by like a hornet, hunting for a bluecoat.

As I know nothing of the movement of other troops, only what I have learned from history, I will confine myself to the 3rd Brigade, until we arrive at Franklin.

The 3rd Brigade drew away from the line at Duck River, with the 2nd Division, at dark on the evening of the 29th, and started for Franklin.

Speaking for myself, I did not know at that time that General Hood was threatening our rear at Spring Hill, and I doubt if there were many in our ranks that did understand the position of the two armies at that time.

As we drew near to Spring Hill, we heard some firing in our front. The 3rd Brigade was at once thrown into line of battle in the fields to the left of the pike, and advanced some distance in that position. Finally, as everything quieted down in front,. Colonel Strickland ordered the brigade by the right flank, and we filed out across the pike into a field to the right, the 50th Ohio being in the lead.

Off to the right of the pike between a quarter and a half mile-was a long string of camp-fires that I supposed were the camps of the 4th Corps. Imagine my surprise then when I learned that they were Confederate camp fires, and here was Scofield's little army marching along, hampered with a long wagon train in good rifle range of their camps, and they were making no effort to stop him.

What did it all mean? Someone was making a huge mistake, but it proved very lucky for us that the mistake was made. But let us go back and follow the 3rd Brigade.

Colonel Strickland, as I have said, led us across the pike into a meadow, and out towards some haystacks, that we could see between us and those camp fires, with the intention, I think, of putting us in line of battle, near those stacks.

The Colonel was riding at the head of the brigade, and as he neared the stacks he was halted by a picket. I did not hear all the conversation that occurred between them, but I did hear Colonel Strickland say: "It's all right, my boy; I want to put my brigade in position here."

A comrade of the 50th, who was near the Colonel and had been listening to the conversation, now spoke up and said, "Colonel, that's a darned rebel you are talking to," and with that the rebel picket fired on us.

Several shots were fired on both sides, and a new regiment just in rear of the 50th, that had been assigned to the 3rd Brigade, became excited and fired a few shots, right up through the 50th, and that caused some little confusion, which soon passed off, and we withdrew from the meadow into the pike and resumed our march toward Franklin.

I never learned whether Colonel Strickland had orders from; his superiors to place the 3rd Brigade in line of battle by those stacks, or whether he was taking us there on his own responsibility.

I did not see any other Union troops nearer than the pike. Two hostile armies are rarely situated as were Hood's and Scofield's that night at Spring Hill, Tennessee.

General Hood had been maneuvering and watching for a chance to throw his army in the rear of Scofield and cut off his line of retreat ever since his advance northward from Florence, Alabama, and now the longed-for opportunity had arrived.

He had the greater part of his army at Spring Hill, and it would have been an easy matter, if I understand the situation, to have formed a line of battle in front of Scofield's retreating column and have placed them between two fires, front and rear; but instead of making use of the opportunity he now had, his army was put in bivouac, and from all appearance were sleeping soundly, while along the pike but a few hundred yards distant tramped the weary little army of General Scofield's, handicapped with a long

But General Hood seemed to be under the impression that he had the blue-coats trapped, and so he slept peacefully on, dreaming that all he would have to do in the morning would be to demand Scofield to surrender his army. But imagine his surprise when he awoke and after rubbing the sleep out of his eyes he reached forth, expecting to put his finger down on the Yanks, but found that they, like the Irishman's flea, were not there.

Ah! General Hood, you must have been a sound sleeper, for it is said that some of the Yanks lit their pipes at your camp fire that night, but be that as it may, you slept away your golden opportunity.

You have nothing to show for the strenuous efforts you made to bag Scofield's army but the skeletons of a few burnt wagons that forest men captured and burned.

Without meeting with anymore adventures, the 3rd Brigade marched on into Franklin, where we arrived about sunrise. We were halted, and after getting breakfast were placed in line of battle, the 50th Ohio being on the left of the brigade.

The left of our regiment rested on the Columbia and Franklin pike. We were immediately put to work, building breastworks. A little to the right of our regiment was a grove of young locust trees, and we used some of the brush in front of our works. Immediately in front of our regiment, and also to the left of the pike, in front of General Riley's brigade, was a clear field nearly a half mile across, without a brush, stump, tree or stone to protect an enemy advancing on us.

Our line of battle ran from the Harpeth River above the town of Franklin, on our left; to the Harpeth River below the town, on our right. The main line of battle was manned by the troops of the 23rd Corps, except on the right below town, where there was some of the 4th Corps placed in position.

Also the batteries in line were from the 4th Corps, as I think the 23rd Corps batteries were all sent across the river. The 4th Corps troops were rear guards from Spring Hill to Franklin.

Directly after noon rations were issued to the 50th, and, if I remember rightly. Company "K's" rations had not been divided among the men yet, when the battle opened, but were lying in bulk in rubber blankets back of our works.

While encamped back at Columbia, Comrade Alexander McCradie of Company "K" was detailed as a safe guard for a citizen of Columbia, but when we had to fall back, he took his place in the Company again, and while I was busy at work on the rifle pits he had cooked dinner for him and me. And as he had some flour, he had baked up quite a stack of slapjacks, and he and I sat down and ate a hearty meal of slapjacks and molasses, coffee and bacon, and I will say just here that that was the last square meal I got till the following March.

The position of the 50th I have already stated was on the right of the Columbia pike, and if I remember rightly, the Carter house, where General Cox, the commander of the lines that day, had his headquarters, was a little to our right rear. The other regiments of our brigade that day were the 72nd Illinois, who joined us on the right, in the front or main line, the 44th Missouri and the 183rd Ohio, and they were our supports in the second line behind us.

The 44th Missouri and the 72nd Illinois belonged to the Army of the Tennessee, but were temporarily placed under Strickland to fill the places of two regiments of our brigade that were at that time with General Cooper at Centerville.

The 183rd Ohio was a new regiment that had just come out, and was also placed under Strickland's command, so that the 50th Ohio was the only regiment of the original 3rd Brigade present.

As soon as General Hood realized at Spring Hill the morning of the 30th that Scofield's army had passed him in the night, he started his army in rapid pursuit, but the 4th Corps troops skirmished with them, and held them in check until late in the afternoon, when all the 4th Corps had come within the lines, except Conrad's and Lane's brigades of Wagner's division.

Those two brigades were placed in line a quarter of a mile in our front, Conrad's on the left of the Columbia pike, and Lane's on the right. That placed Colonel Lane's brigade in front of our 3rd Brigade.

There were also two guns of a battery, with those brigades in front. From history I have learned that Kimball's Division of the 4th Corps, consisting of three brigades, was our extreme right flank below town, resting on the river, and Opdycke's brigade of Wagner's division had come within the lines and were held as a reserve back of our second line. We have already seen where Lane's and Conrad's brigades were.

The balance of the 4th Corps crossed the river and went into line on the north side to protect the crossings. Such was the situation late in the afternoon when we in the main line saw the enemy begin forming for attack in front of Lane's and Conrad's brigades.

The afternoon was clear and the sun was shining brightly, and as the Johnnies wheeled into line and took their position we could see their murderous guns glistening in the bright November sunshine like polished silver.

BATTLE OF FRANKLIN

The Battle of Franklin on November 30, 1864 was one of the Confederacy's worst disasters, with nearly thrice the casualties, and a great victory for Union General John M. Schofield.—Ed. 2017

We watched the Confederates file off to their right, their guns at right shoulder shift, and form into line as coolly as though they were going on dress parade.

And we saw them move forward. Mitchell's two guns were playing on them with shell and canister, mowing great gaps in their ranks, which they immediately closed up and came on.

Finally the cannoneers wound up with a charge of canister, limbered up and came in. General Cox* says they came in at a leisurely trot, but if my eyesight and memory are not at fault they came in with their horses on the lope, and when they had reached about half way from where they had been in line to our main works, the rebs fired a solid shot at them that struck the pike just behind them, and the ball went bounding over our heads into town.

General Jacob Dolson Cox (1828–1900) was a prolific writer after the war. His books on the Atlanta Campaign and Sherman's March are considered classics. The latter included the Battles of Nashville and Franklin.—Ed. 2017

It was a good line shot, but fell a little short.

All eyes were focused on Lane's and Conrad's brigades when the rebs began to advance, expecting them to , retire within our lines and give us a clear field, as we all expected them to do, and as they should have done.

But alas! sad to relate, someone had blundered again, and those poor, brave boys were kept out there firing on the enemy until they were almost surrounded, and when they did start to retire, it was too late, as the enemy were swarming among them.

The rebs, quick to see their advantage, raised the cry, "Let's go in with them; let's go in with them," and so the rush for the center of our main line became a confused mass of blue and grey, wedge-shape, entering our works at the pike, and pressing outward to right and left of the pike, overwhelming the 50th Ohio and a part of Reiley's brigade.

Reiley's line was immediately restored by his troops rallying and charging back from his second line, but the rebels held the line taken from the 50th Ohio till the end of the fight.

Sixty of the 50th Ohio were surrounded and captured in the front line by the rebs; the balance of the regiment rallied in the second line and fought bravely on till the close of the battle.

Many of those brave boys out in front were killed and wounded in the mad rush for our lines, and a number captured.

The reader will remember that at the opening of the battle Opdycke's brigade of the 4th Corps was lying in reserve in rear of both lines.

History tells us that when the break occurred at the center he led his gallant brigade forward and did heroic service in helping to clear the enemy out, that had got between our first and second lines, and I have no doubt that they did.

Some writers have gone so far as to say that it was Opdycke's brigade that saved the day at Franklin. Now, while I am perfectly willing to give those brave men all the credit that is due them for their noble service they rendered that evening, yet I do say without fear of contradiction that I think the day would have been saved if Opdycke's brigade had not been there, for I do not think the enemy would have been able to have broken entirely through the second line, for as far as I can find out, the second line stood firm, and those that left the main line rallied there and fought with them.

Besides, I have no doubt that quite a number from Lane's and Conrad's unfortunate brigades stopped at the second line and fought until the danger at the center was over. Quite a large number of the enemy got in the open space between the two lines in the front of the Carter house, but a deadly fire from the second line, where the 44th Missouri and 83rd Ohio were, and where the 50th Ohio had rallied also, soon cleared them out.

I know this to be the fact by being in a position where I could see it with my own eyes. I stoutly maintain, and always have, that had those two brigades withdrawn within the lines when they saw the enemy forming to charge, and given us a clear field, the rebs would not have broken our lines at the center.

Why did they not break our lines on the right and left flanks? For the simple reason that our troops there did not have to contend with the confusion that we did. They had a clear field for it, where we in the center dared not fire till our troops got in, and then it was too late, as the rebs came right in with them, and simply overwhelmed us.

I shall now give the reader a little of my own personal experience. I had stood and watched the rebs form into line for the charge; had seen Mitchell's two guns come in, and was now watching those two brigades in front; saw the smoke of their muskets as they fired into the faces of the advancing enemy. Saw them break for our lines with the grey coats right among them. From that on till they reached our lines it was a confused mass of blue and grey, in a mad rush for our lines.

Rebel flags and Union flags were fluttering in the breeze; rebel officers were waving their swords and calling their men to come on. Away on our left the ball had already opened; the crash of musketry and the boom of artillery and the bursting shells could be plainly heard above the yelling of the hordes in our front.

But now, see, they have reached our lines; they swarm through the works on the pike, and over the works on top of us, Yank and reb together. I heard Lieutenant Pine say: "Boys, we have got to get out of here." A glance shows me the colors going back; I think it's time for me to go, but ah! I am too late; a big Johnnie Reb, with musket pointed at me, that looks as large to my eyes as a twelve-pound cannon, says: "Yank, I'll take care of you," so that settles the business for me.

My captor and I got down low in the ditch to avoid the storm of lead, which now beggared to sweep over us from all parts of the compass. A reb jumped upon the works beside a fine-looking young

Confederate officer, brought his musket up to his face and fired at Pete Pecheny, our Sergeant Major, his ball cutting the Sergeant across the bridge of his nose.

This enraged the young officer, and he said to the man: "If I see you do another cowardly trick as that, I will cut you down in your tracks with my sword—firing on a man after he has surrendered."

The officer jumped down, took a few steps toward the Carter house, turned and flourished his sword, and urged his men to come on, and then fell, pierced by a Yankee bullet.

Now the music was by the full band on all parts of the line. Pandemonium reigned supreme, and in almost less time than it takes me to relate it, the space between the two lines was cleared of everything, except dead and wounded soldiers.

The crashes of musketry exceeded any that I heard in front of Atlanta, Georgia. One wounded rebel fell on my feet and another on my left shoulder, their life's blood soaking and staining my clothing to the skin.

The enemy clung stubbornly to the outside of the works, out of which they had lifted the 50th Ohio. The prisoners and their captors occupied the inside. After dark the rebs ordered us all to get over on their side. The first time, my captor and I kept quiet, but the second time they threatened to fire on us if we did not come over, so then my captor said we would have to get over, and we did, and I want to say we were not long about it, either, for our second line were keeping up a deadly fire on those works from three directions, so you may judge it was not very healthy on top of those works at that time.

If it had not been for my captor, I would have remained where I was, as the ditch was full of wounded rebs, and being dark, I knew they would not fire into that ditch, for fear of killing their wounded.

But my guard still had his twelve-pounder, and I thought perhaps he might use it on me if I were stubborn, so I hustled over with him. Then he left me, and he may have been killed for aught I know, as I saw him no more. I lay down beside a wounded Confederate Captain.

The rebs in the line soon dwindled down to a mere skirmish line, and they were using the cartridges taken from the boxes of their dead and wounded comrades. The oblique fire from our lines had thinned them out rapidly.

Word was passed along the line for the commanding officer of their brigade, and word came back that he was dead or wounded. Word was passed for the next ranking officer, and received the same answer, and this was repeated with like results until it reached the wounded Captain by my side. Then he spoke up, and said: "Men, this won't do; we must either surrender or run" but it seemed sure death to attempt to cross that field at that time, as the boys in blue were sending a death-dealing storm of leaden hail across it from right, left and front.

The Captain said again: "Men, won't some of you please hoist a white flag? If I were able to get up, I would do it myself, for we are getting all cut to pieces by this terrible cross-fire." But his men did not heed what he said, but still kept firing.

I felt very much like I would love to do the Captain that little favor if I only dared, for I knew I was in great danger of being killed by my own comrades, as I was lying on the bank back of the works, and could hear the balls strike the wounded that were lying near me.

When the Captain realized that his wishes were not being complied with, he hollowed three or four times at the top of his voice: "We surrender; we surrender; we surrender," but of course our men did not hear him, for they were making too much racket themselves.

Now, reader, if you happen to be a comrade, perhaps you can imagine my feelings at this time. I was a prisoner of war in the power of a mere handful of the enemy, while within a stone's throw of me were hundreds of my friends and comrades, and yet I could not get to them.

Visions of Andersonville Castle, Thunder and Libby prisons passed in panoramic view before me, and oh! how I wished that I could get to Colonel Strickland and tell him the facts, as I knew they existed; had I now been on the other side of the works, I certainly would have tried to crawl to our lines.

Surely, I thought, bur men will certainly come back and retake this line; and realizing if they did I was in a very dangerous position where I was, I crawled up to the works, picking up a rebel blanket on my way, and wrapping it around me, lay up against the earthworks as close as possible, and waited for developments.

I heard the rebs make two or three charges on their left, but I did not know if they were successful or not.

I had marched all the night before, worked nearly all day, and now fatigue began to tell on me. Laying up against that clay bank with the messengers of death buzzing over my head, I forgot my troubles, and fell asleep.

How long I slept I do not know, but when I awoke there was not a gun firing along the entire line. A few of my friends, the enemy, were still holding the line. I got up and crawled over the works on what had been our side at the beginning of the battle. One of the rebs asked me where I was going. I do not remember what reply I made him. It was very dark, and I suppose he thought I was one of his comrades, as he paid me no further attention.

I walked on in the direction of what I supposed was the Carter house, and I came do a man leaning with his arms on a paling fence, I think it was. I took him to be a citizen, as he had on a white shirt, and the white shirt bosom was what drew my attention to him, as it shone quite plainly in the dark.

I went to him and inquired if the Yankees were all gone, but he did not seem to want to talk, and finding I could get no direct answer out of him, I walked out to the pike and started down into town.

I did not get far before I met Mr. Johnnie Reb. He was unarmed, and so was I. We began to question each other, and I am afraid that neither one of us was particular to stick close to the truth in our answers. However, Johnnie seemed to suspect me. He would not pass me at close quarters, but flanked out into, the middle of the pike and passed on.

I did not get much further until I ran afoul of the patrol guards from the rebel General Brown's division, and as I thought it would not be good military tactics for one unarmed Yank to tackle Hood's army, though he only had a remnant left, I surrendered the second time for that night, with as good grace as I possibly could.

They took me back through what had been our lines, and as we passed through on the pike it was quite dark, but I glanced to the right and left where the fight had been severe, and as far as my eye could penetrate through the darkness, and it seemed , to me as though the dead were lying in heaps.

We passed on out the Columbia pike over the battlefield to a stone fence on the right of the pike, and we passed inside the fence, where they had a large fire, and around which I found several others of my comrades.

The reader will naturally ask the question. Why was not this part of the line retaken, as well as the part that Reilly's men were driven out of at first?

General Cox says in his history of the Battle of Franklin that he had Colonel Bond's regiment, 112th Illinois, brought from the left to aid Colonel Strickland to re-establish the line, sometime after dark, and that an attempt was made to retake it, but the oblique fire by our men from the second line, both right and left, was so deadly across the space between the two lines that it made the front line untenable, although word had been sent to those troops on right and left to cease firing.

But the din of battle made it hard to get orders understood by the men in line, and they could not be restrained from firing obliquely at the flash of the enemy's guns. And that Colonel Bond was wounded twice slightly by our own troops, so that they withdrew and waited a more favorable opportunity, which it appears never came; hence we prisoners who had been taken in the confusion of the first dash on the center were left to our fate.

I want to put it on record here that there was no time after the first charge of the enemy, but what that line could have been retaken, especially after dark, as there was nothing left there then but a mere skirmish line with us prisoners.

I know what I am talking about, for I was right there, and understood the situation. If the line had been retaken there would have been at least about seventy-five prisoners released.

I shall never forget the humming, dismal sound of these messengers of death, as they passed over me and went whizzing over that field of blood, as I lay there a prisoner that night between the two lines of battle.

I can also vouch for that deadly crossfire that General Cox speaks of, for I could hear the balls striking our camp kettles and coffee pots that were back of our works, showing that the boys were obeying the standing order-—when going into battle, to fire low.

The balls came so thick from our second line just after I was captured that it seemed to me had I held up my little finger it would have been shot away. Is it any wonder then that the space between the lines was so speedily cleared out?

Just at that time the battle was raging furiously; cannon were booming, shells were bursting, and the crash of musketry was deafening; thousands of men were engaged in a struggle for victory; men were dying, and men were being maimed for life. Blood was being poured out as freely as water.

Truly, General Sherman could not have given a better definition of war than he did, had he searched all through the English language. For the time it lasted, and the number of men engaged, the Battle of Franklin, Tennessee, can well be recorded in history as one of the bloodiest battles of the war of the rebellion.

I here give General Cox's estimate of the forces present on both sides, and the loss that each sustained during the battle: Confederates present, 22,000; loss, buried on the field, 1,750; wounded and placed in hospitals in Franklin, 3,800; taken prisoners, 702; total loss, 6,252. Federals present, 23,734; loss, killed, 189; wounded, 1,033; missing, 1, 104; total loss, 2,326.

The Confederate loss in general officers was quite heavy, five being killed, namely: Major General Cleburne, Brigadier Generals Adams, Gist, Strahl and Granbury; six wounded, namely: Major General John C. Brown, Brigadier General Carter, Manigault, Quarles, Cockrell and Scott, and Brigadier General Gordon captured.

That there were so many general officers killed and wounded speaks well for their courage and bravery. It shows they did not shirk their duty in time of danger.

If General Hood had not brought on the fight at Franklin he could have had the town next morning without the loss of a man, as General Scofield merely made a stand there to save his wagon train. His intention was to withdraw the army from Franklin at dark and proceed to Nashville, but Hood's attack, of course, changed that part of the program. However, at midnight, the battle being over, Scofield withdrew and led his army towards Nashville, and Hood, with his badly cut-up army, limped along after him in a few hours. To sum up the matter, two mistakes were made in this campaign. Hood made a blunder at Spring Hill in not striking Scofield when he had the opportunity, and someone made a big mistake at Franklin in keeping those brigades out in front of us too long.

It might have caused us to suffer a disastrous defeat. It was a bad beginning, but rounded up all right for our side in the end, except those of us who were prisoners.

We were up against a hard proposition, and it did not take us very long to realize it. That night after we got back around the prisoners' fire, the rebs seemed very much elated, boasting what they had done, and what they were going to do. They really seemed to think they had won quite a victory.

They told me they were going on to take Nashville and Louisville, and in reply I told them they would run against a snag before they got Nashville, not to mention Louisville, and I am under the impression that they found out that I was right in the wind-up.

When daylight came, and they began to find out the heavy losses they had met with, they looked pretty blue over it. That put a stop to their boasting.

General Hood had a mania for rushing his men into slaughter pens, and he certainly had it bad at Franklin, November 30th, 1864.

HOW WE FARED UNDER THE STARS AND BARS

I have told in the preceding chapter how at the beginning of the confusion in the center, one glance showed me our colors starting for the second line, but just at that moment my whole attention was drawn to that Johnnie Reb with the big gun, so I did not get to see what was taking place around the flag.. But since the war I have seen and talked with Comrade Joseph Chamberlain of Company "K," who was our color bearer at that time, and he as well as other comrades have told me how near he came to losing the colors, as well as his life, when the break occurred.

He says that when he saw we would have to fall back he started for the second line, with the rebs in hot pursuit. One in particular, more fleet than the others, yelled at Chamberlain two or three times, "'Drop that flag, you Yankee son-of-a-gun," and in another second would have run his bayonet through Chamberlain, but just at that moment one of the color guard came to the rescue, fired on Mr. Johnnie, and he fell. Thus was Chamberlain saved, as well as the colors.

This took place between the first and second line, and not far from the second line. This Chamberlain told me himself, that the

Johnnie would have got him if it had not been for the color guard downing the reb just in the nick of time. This goes to show how determined the Confederates were.

The little break at the center deceived them for a while. They thought they had the Yankees whipped, but before midnight they found out their mistake.

Company "K" captured a Confederate flag that evening at Franklin, but foolishly gave it up to a soldier of some other command, thus losing the credit for its capture.

Corporal Henry Fox of Company "K" was the man that captured it, but in the rush for it the rebs shot him in the left arm, disabling him, so that he handed the flag to Coleman Quinn of Company "K," who it seems did not understand there was any honor connected with a captured flag, so that when another soldier asked him for the flag, he handed it over to him without a word, thus depriving Company "K" of an honor that should have been hers. No doubt the soldier that got the flag told some big story of how he captured it from the enemy.

This happened also close to our second line, and not far from the pike. The rebs ordered Fox to drop the flag and surrender, but he refused, and lost his left arm by it.

Corporal Fox was a good soldier, and so was Quinn, and I am very sorry that they lost the credit of capturing that flag. Someone asked Quinn why he gave it away, and he said he had no use for that old rag.

Of course I did not see this, but those that told me were eyewitnesses, so I will vouch for it being true.

The Confederates were brave and fearless, and the fighting they put up was worthy of a better cause.

As this ended my service with Company "K" and the 50th Ohio, I will here give a short sketch of their service from Franklin till their muster-out, as I have been told by other Comrades, and then bid them good-bye, and proceed to tell my own experience from Franklin till the 21st of the following May, naming other comrades as I pass along that I was closely connected with, during that very eventful period of my life.

The 50th Ohio still remained in the ring, although their numbers were somewhat reduced after the Battle of Franklin.

They withdrew with the balance of the army to Nashville, Tennessee, and took a part in helping to reduce General Flood's army to a frazzle, and joined in pursuing the straggling remnant of it across the Tennessee River.

Lieutenant Pine of Company "K" was wounded at Nashville, from the effects of which he died in a few days. He was a brave officer, and was highly esteemed by both officers and privates. The community in which he resided at the time of his enlistment lost a good citizen and a noble Christian gentleman.

At his death he left a wife and two children to mourn his untimely death. He was cut down in the prime of his manhood. In his church at home he was the leader in song, both in the church and Sunday-school, so he was sadly missed by a large circle of friends at home, as well as in the army.

But he was not the only one that was cut down by the deadly bullets that had the promise of a brilliant future before them. Hundreds, yes thousands of young men, both in the South, as well as the North, had their lives snuffed out in the prime of young manhood, who, had they lived, would have made their mark in the world.

Oh! when will men cease to war with each other? And learn to love peace?

The Battle of Nashville was the last battle that the 50th Ohio took any part in. They followed the remnant of Hood's army back across the Tennessee River, and at Clifton, Tennessee, the 50th and the 99th Ohio were consolidated, both being small regiments, but were known from that on as the 50th Ohio.

They were then put aboard a steamboat and shipped to Cincinnati; then sent by B. & O. Railroad to Washington, D. C., about January 20th, 1865, crossing over the long bridge, and went to Camp Stoneman, where Company "'D" presented Captain Carnahan of their company a fine sword and revolver.

From thence they were shipped to Wilmington, North Carolina, where they arrived about the 1st of March; then they marched to Kingston and Goldsborough, where they met General Sherman's army, that had just arrived from Savannah.

This was the first they had seen of any of Sherman's army since they parted in Georgia in the month of October, 1864, the 50th coming back into Tennessee with the 23rd and 4th Corps, and Sherman starting on his famous [march to the sea](), and then up through the swamps to Goldsborough, North Carolina.

The meeting was an enthusiastic one. The boys were all glad to see their favorite General once more. They were about here somewhere when Lee and Johns[t]on surrendered, and joined in the grand jubilee on that occasion.

The 50th was sent to Saulsbury about this time, and while hunting for water in the night were fired on by the citizens from some of the houses, and a number were wounded. Several arrests were made at the time.

It was at Saulsbury, June 26th, that the regiment was mustered out of the service and sent by the way of Pittsburg to Camp Cleveland, Ohio, and from thence to Camp Denison, Ohio, where, on the 17th of July, they were paid off, discharged and sent home. Thus ended the service of the 50th Ohio Regiment.

While they are not numbered in Fox's fighting regiments, they tried to do what they were ordered to do, and to go wherever they were ordered to go, and this was all that was required of any regiment in the service.

Their loss was 76 killed in battle and 134 died of disease. Being at home when the regiment came to Camp Denison, I went there and saw them and stayed one night with them, but there were so many of the poor boys missing that it was rather a sad meeting. What few of my comrades were left gave me a warm greeting.

Some of them that I saw then and bade them good-bye I have never seen since, and never expect to see them now, till we all meet in that grandest of grand reunions, over the dark river, where God Himself shall be the Supreme Commander.

Many of those that left friends and homes as I did in 1862 are sleeping in unknown graves. Some sleep in the Dark and Bloody Ground of Kentucky, some in fair Tennessee and Georgia, and still others rest on the slimy bottom of the Mississippi River.

A few of us still live at this writing, June 12th, 1905, but our numbers are few; our heads are blossoming for the grave.

When a few of us old comrades chance to meet now and then we have jolly good times, rehearsing what we passed through from 1861 to 1865.

There is a bond between old comrades that nothing but death can sever, and if we cheer when we see the old Stars and Stripes floating on high, who has a better right?

A TOUGH MARCH

And now, kind reader, as I have taken leave of Company "K" and the 50th Ohio, let us go back and gather up my end of the thread again, which from now on we will find full of knots and tangles.

In a day or two after the Battle of Franklin the Confederates had us prisoners back in the old fort at Columbia. On our way here we met quite a number of stragglers from General Hood's army, tramping along toward Franklin.

One among the number took a fancy to a new hat I was wearing at the time, and as I passed him he made a desperate grab for it, but fortunately he missed it. The guard that was my escort at the time gave him to understand in plain language that I was in his care, and that he did not intend that I should be robbed, while he had charge of me; and further told him his place was up in front, where he would find something else to do besides insulting and robbing prisoners. That was about all that happened worthy of note till we arrived at Columbia, but fearing now I would lose my new hat, I traded it off to a Johnnie for his old one and some cornbread.

I found among the prisoners the following comrades from Company "K": Andrew J. Punder, Andrew J. Culp, Alexander McCradie, Peter Shilling and Henry Venant. Comrade McCradie had been detailed as a safe guard for a gentleman living in Columbia before our retreat, but had come back to the company when we began to fall back.

McCradie now said to me: "I wish I could see Mr.—. I believe he would get me out of here." And as the citizens visited the fort each day to look at us tame Yanks, McCradie had the good fortune one day of seeing the gentleman, and sure enough he got McCradie out, and took him home with him, and he remained there till after Hood's defeat at Nashville and watched from an upper window and saw the boys in blue take the boys in grey, whirling back through Columbia on their way to Dixie.

After McCradie's discharge from the army, he stayed with this gentleman two years, and had one of his sisters down there awhile.

It was lucky for McCradie, seeing the man, as it saved him going to prison with us.

When McCradie learned he was to be taken away from us, he gave me his blanket—or rather, what was left of it. At the Battle of Franklin it had been neatly folded and laid in our rear, just back of our line, and being in that open space between the two lines of battle, it had suffered accordingly.

There was hardly a space in it as large as my two hands but what had been riddled with bullets, but I accepted it gladly, and kept it during my imprisonment. He also gave Comrade Pouder and me his spoon and a three-quart tin bucket that he had bought from a colored man at Columbia. That bucket was treasured by Pouder and me, and it proved to be very convenient for us while in prison, and you may be sure that Comrade Punder and I were very thankful to Comrade McCradie for his thoughtful kindness in willing us such a useful article at that time. I hardly know what Pouder and I would have done without it. That three-quart bucket will come to the front several times in these reminiscences.

Watch for it.

We had a pretty cold time of it in the old fort. We scarcely got wood enough to cook our scanty rations of cornmeal which the Johnnies doled out to us.

We remained till the 14th of December, when we were started out on the march toward Cherokee Station, Alabama, which place we reached on the 21st, being on the tramp eight days. This was one of the hardest marches that I ever made. We had all kinds of weather during the time, but rain rather predominated; mud, water and slush was ankle deep. I make no doubt but what quite a number of the poor boys gave out and were shot by the guards on the way, as, it was a common incident to hear the report of muskets back in the rear.

Some of the guards were kind-hearted, but it did no good for them to remonstrate with those that were not.

I saw an incident of that kind one day. One guard rebuked another for abusing one of the prisoners, who was just about given out; the two guards quarreled about it and drew their guns on each other, and for a short time it looked as though they would fire on each other, but finally they separated. What became of the poor prisoner I never knew, but I am satisfied he never got very much further on the road, for it was impossible for him to keep up.

I am very thankful that God gave me strength to keep in my place. A few of the prisoners made their escape on this march; among the number were two commissioned officers of the 50th Ohio; they made their escape in safety, and were welcomed into our lines a few days later.

One of them had been acting as commissary for the prisoners since our capture, but when they called for him to come and draw our rations one evening, he was found to be missing.

I call to mind one night we camped in the woods, and after we had eaten our cornmeal gruel and my comrade Pouder and I were making our bed for the night, we noticed two comrades prepare their bed pretty near the guard line, but we thought nothing of it at the time, but Just as, we were about to drop off to sleep we heard a great racket, and the guards on our side of camp opened fire.

Pouder and I raised up to see what the trouble was, and we found that those two comrades had made a break for freedom. I could never learn whether they escaped or not, but think quite likely they did. That would have been the time for Pouder and I to have made a run for it, while the guards' guns on our side of camp were empty, but we failed to see and grasp the opportunity until it was too late. ,

After crossing the Tennessee River, we went into camp on the south bank. It had been raining, but turned colder, and there was a little snow fell. There were guards stationed around us from the river above to the river below us, but none between us and the river.

The Confederates allowed us axes to get wood, as the weather had turned cold so suddenly, and our clothes being wet the change was pretty severe for us. However, having the axes, we soon had pretty good fires going.

Some of us boys talked of making a raft and trying to float by the guards below us, but the weather was so cold we abandoned the idea. If the weather had been warmer, I believe some of us could have made a success of it, for if I mistake not, we had gunboats below us on the Tennessee River at that time.

In one way the night favored us, for it was as dark as a stack of black cats; one could see no distance out on the river but we were afraid of perishing with the cold, and did not make the attempt, and perhaps it is just as well we did not.

Being very hungry while here, I gathered up some shelled corn off the ground, that some horse or mule had slobbered over, washed it, put it in the three-quart bucket, boiled it and ate it, but I found it pretty tough chewing. It made my jaws tired. However, it did to fill up on.

Pouder and I made our bed that night on a brush pile, and during the night the river rose, and in the morning when we awoke we found the water all up under our bed. If the night had been an hour longer the water would have reached our bodies.

At Cherokee Station we were put aboard platform cars, and after a very slow run we arrived at Corinth, Mississippi, on the morning of the 23rd of December. Part of this run, as I now remember it, was made in the night, and as the weather was cold we suffered a great deal from the exposure of riding on the open cars.

I judge it was hard for them to keep up steam, for they would stop every little while from some cause; I don't know what for, unless it was for want of steam. Whenever they would make one of those stops we would all jump off the cars, and the guards would kindle fires. If they could find nothing else to burn, they would set fire to the broom sage grass along the road and that would blaze up and throw out a little warmth, enough to keep us from freezing.

The guards really did not seem to pay much attention to us, and I know I thought it would be an easy matter to give them the slip, but I don't believe any of the boys tried it. If they did, I heard nothing about it. It was rather too cold to make the attempt.

When I look back through the years to that memorable march from Columbia, Tennessee, to Cherokee, Alabama [about 100 miles/161 km], through the mud, snow and rain in the bleak month of December, 1864, I wonder how I ever kept up in my place in the ranks. Then, too, the exposure of riding on platform cars from Cherokee to Corinth that bitter cold night—it was certainly very trying on the nerves.

But I was in the heyday of youth, and was in the best of health.

Coupled with this, I felt that our cause was just and right, and never for a moment doubted but what we would conquer in the end. A something within me seemed to say: "Do not give up; do not despair; bear your burdens bravely; keep in good heart and spirits; you shall yet be welcomed back into the family circle. Put your trust in God; do not let these trials overwhelm you; your life is in God's hands, and is safe."

Thus was I buoyed up with hope, and never once doubted but what I would return in safety to my old Kentucky home.

But many of the poor boys did not have this hope within them and gave way to grief and homesickness, and the trials and hardships that came to them soon took them over the Dark River of Death.

We remained at Corinth only one day and night. On December 24th we were put aboard some box cars and shipped to Meridian, Mississippi, arriving there on Christmas night, spending Christmas Day on the cars, and our Christmas dinner was raw corn, of which there was plenty at the stations along the road, we found it a very poor substitute for turkey.

At Meridian we were placed in a stockade, with guards thrown around us. We fared very well here. We drew a quart of cornmeal for a day's ration; drew a little beef or pork; some days, spare ribs and a few black peas.

I had gotten hold of some Confederate money, and when we got the spare ribs I bought some sweet potatoes, and baked them in an oven that we drew and we enjoyed eating sweet potatoes and spare ribs immensely.

Sweet potatoes were plentiful here, and we could buy all we wanted from the guards, if we had the money. If I remember rightly, I think we drew a small allowance of chewing tobacco. While here also, two prisoners made their escape by climbing the stockade one night. I do not remember if they succeeded in getting away entirely or not.

Some of the prisoners got the guards interested in a trade, and that gave the two comrades a chance to climb the stockade and make a break for freedom.

This little incident created quite a stir among the Confederate officers and men for a short time, and the outcome was that they were a great deal stricter with us after that.

My third New Year while in the service was spent in Meridian prison. If the reader will take the pains to compare the three, he will find quite a contrast between them.

Some of the prisoners that were captured at Franklin were sent to Andersonville prison. I am very thankful that I escaped going to that awful den. Any of the prisons were bad enough, but some of them were more cruel than others.

While we remained at Meridian, we got along very well.

On the 9th of January, 1865, we were once more put aboard the cars and shipped to Castle Morgan, Cahaba, Alabama, where we arrived on the 12th. I think we went as far as Selma on the cars; remained overnight, and then marched to Cahaba, the next morning being greeted by the cry of "Fresh fish!" as we entered the stockade.

Cahaba is the worst Civil War POW camp you've probably never heard of. A larger percentage of those who left Cahaba died once back in Union lines than of those who left Andersonville.—Ed. 2017

CRUEL TREATMENT

Castle Morgan, the Cahaba prison, was a large double brick building, situated on the west side of the Alabama River, near where the Cahaba River empties into it.

The building was nearly two hundred feet long, and I would judge one hundred and twenty feet wide. It had double doors in the north or up-river end; the walls were fifteen feet high, and only partially covered, a place near the center being left open.

Bunks were placed around the walls that would accommodate six hundred men by tight squeezing; the remaining two thousand five hundred men that were there that winter had to sleep on the ground.

Our water supply, I am glad to say, was abundant, and I thought pure. It came from an artesian well not far from the prison, being led to the center of the building underground by covered wooden troughs. It came up in the prison into a large wooden trough, or rather box that we used for drinking and cooking purposes. Then it passed out of that into another box, where we washed our hands and faces from. Thence it was led through our closet vaults, and then out into the river.

The water, of course, when first dipped up was too warm to be palatable, but after setting in a vessel for a while, was very refreshing to one that was thirsty. It was delightful water to bathe the hands and face in on a cold morning.

A wrong impression has been made on the minds of many about our water supply. By reading a book published by a Dr. Hawes* some years ago, in describing our water supply, he says that it came from an artesian well in the town of Cahaba, and was led to the prison through open gutters, thereby receiving on its way the filth of the streets. He seems to base his knowledge on the report of the Confederate surgeon, R. M. Whitfield, which was found in the Confederate archives.

CAHABA: Captive Boys in Blue by Dr. Jesse Hawes.

The report said that the water in its course to the prison was subjected to the washing of hands, feet, faces and heals of soldiers, citizens and Negroes, and in it were rinsed buckets, tubs and spittoons of groceries, offices and hospitals, and that in it could be 'found the filth from hogs, cows and horses, as well as from the streets and other sources.

But I have lately seen and conversed with Dr. Howard Henderson, who at this date, July, 1905, is living at Hartwell, Ohio. He contradicts the above statement, and tells me that there was a large artesian well in the town, but our water supply came from a smaller well, not far from the prison, and that it was led underground to the prison in covered wooden troughs, and I am willing to take General Henderson's word, as I don't think he is the man to wish to misrepresent the matter, but I give the reader both statements to choose from. That's the best I can do, as I never got out to see for myself.

While I was there, I was out of the stockade once during my imprisonment, but I went out for wood, and got no farther than the wood yard. But I will say that while I knew the water was warm, still while I was there I always supposed it to be free from impurity:

Our rations consisted of about two-thirds of a pint of cornmeal ground, cob and all, and very coarse at that, and a small piece of bacon, or a small piece of fresh beef per man for a day, and at very rare intervals we would be given a few Negro peas that were full of bugs. How would you like this fare, you well-to-do Americans?—who call the veterans who saved this country for you, "Government paupers"

A stockade of heavy planks or timbers was built around the prison, being set in the ground three or four feet, and reaching above ground twelve or fifteen feet. A walk was placed on the outside of the stockade near the top, where guards paced day and night. This stockade was far enough away from the building on the north side to afford us room for a cook yard; while, if I remember rightly, on the south and east sides, the stockade was only about ten or twelve feet from the building.

There was a door or gateway near the northwest corner of the stockade, and on the north side two pieces of artillery standing ready to carry death and destruction into our ranks if we should make a break for freedom.

Six feet from the stockade inside was the dead line, so called from the fact that if a prisoner stepped across it the guards had orders to kill him.

About every ten or twelve men had a skillet issued to them, in which to cook their scant rations. One man out of ten would be allowed to pass out after wood once in ten days, and what he could carry in his arms, or on his shoulder. This one trip would have to run his squad the ten days.

Such is a brief description of the vile den that we turned into that 12th day of January, 1865. Truly our misery now commenced in dead earnest.

General Howard Henderson had been in charge of the prison the summer before we came in, but he had been promoted to General and Commissioner of Exchange, and now Major or Colonel Jones was in command.

There was a wide difference in the two men. General Henderson was kind, and did what he could to better the condition of the prisoners, while Jones was heartless and brutal, and did not let an opportunity pass to show his bitter hatred of the poor prisoners who were so unfortunate as to come under his charge.

It has been told of him that he said on one occasion: "I am sorry that the damned blue-bellied Yankees are so tough. They don't die fast enough. If I could have, my way, I would hang every devil of them."

I have never met a Cahaba prisoner but what spoke well of General Henderson, but were very bitter against Major Jones.

Before we entered Cahaba, we were all searched, and had to give up all moneys, watches or other valuables we had; they told us that all those things would be put in a safe and when we left there everything would be returned to us again. I never learned whether they kept their promise or not.

I had a five-dollar Confederate bill that I turned over to them, but I got that back in checks a few days afterwards, and speculated on it, buying bread from the prison sutler and selling it to the prisoners again at a profit, thus making my own bread free.

There were so many little smoky fires in our cook yard that some of the men were almost blind from the smoke. No axes were given us to chop up our wood; a railroad spike had to fill the place of ax and wedge, and a billet of wood did service as a mall.

So a request that we often heard was: "Partner, will you loan me your spike to split up some wood?" A spike was prized very highly, and they were kept brightly polished by their constant use.

The wood we got was mostly green pine, and made more smoke than it did fire, and required someone to continually fan it with an old hat to cause it to make heat enough to cook our corn.

A number of the prisoners made mush out of their meal and ate it that way, but the five of us Company "K" boys had managed some way (I cannot remember how at this late date) to get possession of a smoothing iron heater, and that we used to bake our bread in.

Here is where our three-quart bucket came in good play. We used it to mix our cornmeal in, and also to make mush in. We did not pretend to eat only once a day and that could not be called a meal; it was only a mere taste.

We would bake a cake in our iron heater, and then I would cut it into five equal parts, and then one of the five would turn his back, and the cook would point to a piece and ask whose it was, and the comrade with his back turned would call out the name, and this was repeated until each one got his share. This plan generally gave satisfaction.

The rations were so very scant that we had to use great care in order that each one would get his portion.

My mess of five agreed to be kind of saving with our meal and try to get enough ahead, so we could cook two meals a day, and about the time we were ready for that luxury some thief stole our meal, so that put an end to that plan.

There was stealing going on all the time; the thieves in there would steal anything that was loose. They would steal blankets off of each other at nights, and would almost steal the shoes off your feet; in fact, if you wished to keep what little you had you were compelled to make it fast to your body, or have someone watch it night and day.

We were all given warning of the dead line before we passed into the stockade, and as a general thing we gave it a wide berth, but one evening just before dark I got permission with two or three others to cross it, and pull some dry slivers off the stockade.

But the guard must have seen some of his officers coming, for just as we got busy getting our slivers he yelled out at us, and wanted to know what we were doing there. We made one jump back on our own side, and I never tried to cross it anymore.

As he was the one that gave us the permission to cross it, he either wanted to see us jump, or saw some officers coming, was the way I accounted for his action.

There was no one shot for crossing the line after our arrival there that winter, but I learned there had been several shot the summer and fall before our coming.

The guards we had that winter were mostly old men and boys. I imagine that some of them were just as strong Union men as we were, it seemed that some of them wished to be humane, and were as far as they dared be; they were simply caught in the trap, and could not help themselves. :

One of the guards by the name of Daniel Boone (I don't know whether he was related to the famous Kentucky trapper or not) said that he was placed on guard one morning on a beat that ran from the doors to the stockade on the river side.

A short time afterwards, as he returned to retrace his beat he found one of the prisoners walking the same beat behind him. He drove him off, and in a short time found the same man walking behind him again, and he said this was repeated three or four times.

Boone said this was the only instance that he felt like shooting a prisoner, but he said he was quite provoked at the time to think the man would act that way, and the only way he could account for the man's actions was that he was discouraged, and had given up all hopes, and wanted Boone to end his misery with a shot from his musket, and I judge that was the true reason.

In the daytime we were allowed out in the cook yard, but at nights we all had to stay inside the old building and two sets of guards were thrown around us, one set inside the building and the other on top of the stockade outside, and it almost seems as though I can hear the familiar call yet of: "Post No. 4, half past two o'clock, and all is well."

The early morning occupation of all who had ambition enough to try to care for themselves was to strip off their clothes and skirmish for graybacks, for in this way only could we manage to keep the little pest from literally eating our bodies raw, for the very dust of old Cahaba was alive with them, and they did not believe in race suicide either, for they were all married and had large families, and they appeared to thrive on Yankee blood, for some of them were large and robust enough to have carried good-sized knapsacks.

The Confederates counted us every morning to see if any of us had gotten away in the night. None escaped that I heard of through the winter.

A great pastime among some of the prisoners was "chuckaluck." They would commence the game soon after daylight and keep it up as long as they could in the evening, and although the Confederates tried hard to get all the money out of the prison, yet I saw quite a number of greenbacks handled by the chuckaluck players, and if I am not badly mistaken there were some fifty and one hundred dollar bills among them.

Those that had no money played for buttons and other trinkets.

The only spot that my squad of five could find to sleep at nights, when it was raining, was used as a path or passway through the day, and black, filthy mud would be worked up to the depth of three or four inches, so that when it came time to lie down one of us would take a chip or something of that kind and scrape away the black ooze down to the solid ground, and then thrown down our old rags and lie down, all facing one way, and lie that way till our hip bones felt as though ready to come through the skin.

And then one of us would hollow "Spoon 1" and then the five of us would flop over on the other side, and thus we would wear the long nights away.

When the weather was fair and no rain falling, we slept out in the open, where there was no roof over us but the sky. Here we had more room, but when it rained, of course we would try to crowd in under shelter.

I don't think we had any snow there that winter, but a great deal of rain fell, and some nights were cold, and we suffered, for a great many of the poor men and boys had no covering.

I think the last prisoners sent there were in a worse condition than were those before us; it looked to me like those that had the bunks were better off, but God knows we all suffered enough.

It has been said that Cahaba was the best prison in the South. Well, if it was, God pity the worst, for I consider that Cahaba was the ragged end of misery, whittled off to a sharp point.

We were permitted to write letters to our friends, but of course they had to be read by those in charge, and if there was nothing contraband in them they were forwarded to their destination. I sent two letters to my people while there, and in order that the reader may know my condition and feelings at that time I shall copy the letters here in full. There is not much news in them, but I was compelled to make them brief and to the point.

While my parents were in deep trouble because I was a prisoner, yet it filled their hearts with joy that they could receive word from me in my own handwriting, and in a measure they were comforted by my apparent cheerfulness.

"Military Prison, Cahaba, Alabama,

"January 14th, 1865.

"My Dear Parents, Brothers and Sisters:

"I seat myself this beautiful day to write you a few lines to let you know where I am at the present time. I suppose you know ere this that I am a prisoner of war.

"I am at present at Cahaba, Alabama; am treated as well, I suppose, as a prisoner can expect to be treated.

"Andrew J. Pouder, son of Leonard Pouder, is with me. We are getting along first rate. We are both in good health and spirits.

"I feel that God is with me, and I have that strong faith that teaches me that He will bring me out all right.

"Tell the folks where I am, and tell them to write me."

"Direct 'Military Prison, Cahaba, Alabama.' Write only on one page. I have filled my limits, and will close with love to all.

"Your affectionate son and brother,

"Erastus Winters."

"Military Prison, Cahaba, Alabama,

"February 10th, 1865.

"Beloved Parents, Brothers and Sisters:

"I take the present time to pencil you a few words to let you know I am still on the land, and among the living, for which I return my sincere thanks to God, who is the maker and giver of all good gifts.

"I have written you once before since I came here, but have received no answer, but of course can put up with it; at least, I have to whether I want to or not. I am still in good health and spirits, and able for my cornbread and sow belly.

"Today the sun shines warm and pleasant. I would love to be out to enjoy the free air of heaven, but it seems to be ordained otherwise.

"I stand ready at all times to be ready to submit to the will of God, knowing He doeth all things well.

"Should you see Leonard Pouder, tell him his son Andrew is with me, and is in good health and spirits.

"Be sure to write, and direct by 'Military Prison, Cahaba, Alabama, by way of Vicksburg, by flag of truce, in care of Colonel Howard Henderson.'

"Tell the folks to write and tell me all the news.

"This leaves me well. May it hasten to those who wait for tidings.

"With love and good wishes for all, I am as ever,

"Your loving son and brother,

"Erastus Winters."

When those letters had been inspected by the proper officers they were enclosed in an envelope made of brown wrapping paper and addressed to my father at Ludlow, Kentucky, and also the words, "Prisoner's letter," were written on upper left-hand corner, then turned over, and the following was written on the flap of the envelope: "Examined and approved, H. O. M. Henderson, Capt. and Acting Com. of Exchange, C. S. A."

They were not sealed, but forwarded and came through O.K. to my father at Ludlow, Ky. I have one of the envelopes yet, and it is quite a relic of the lost cause.

The reader can see by those letters that I kept up my nerve and tried to appear cheerful to the folks at home, while at the same time I was suffering, but being stout and healthy and full of Yankee grit and pluck I would not give way to despair.

It would have been much better for the poor boys if they could all have kept up their courage like this, but, alas! many of them would give away to grief, and did not have the courage to try to better their condition, but would sit down or lie down and not even try to hunt the vermin off themselves, but would allow them to multiply and increase on their bodies until they became so numerous they would suck the very life-blood from their poor, emaciated frames, and they would become weak and sick, be taken to the hospital, where death would soon end their misery.

Reader, you may doubt the truth of this statement, but I affirm before high Heaven that it is the truth. I saw men in Cahaba prison whose backs were eaten raw by the vermin, and the hair of their heads was stiff with them.

These were exceptional case, of course, where the men had given away to despair, and hope had long ago taken its flight from their breast. Ah! these were the days and scenes that tried men's souls. Someone has called this prison "Cruel Cahaba" and no word in the English language could better describe it.

A BREAK IN THE DARK CLOUDS AT LAST

Among three thousand men there are always some odd characters, and we had a few of them in Cahaba.

There was one I remember who could imitate a dog in some ways to perfection. If the boys would toss him a piece of bread he would snap it into his mouth the same as a dog. It was quite interesting and laughable to watch him.

Then there was a big, hearty, jolly Sergeant that was always seemingly in a good humor, who kept his mess in pretty fair shape, as he always tried to keep something of a laughable nature before their minds, and did not allow them to become discouraged and hopeless.

"By Mighty" was his by-word, and "By Mighty" was the name he was known by in the prison.

There was one squad that would get together of an evening and pass away an hour or so singing songs. Among their favorite songs was "The Yellow Rose of Texas," and another about some chap named Jimmie that had been drafted into the army.

It was well that we had some such characters with us. They put a little spirit into us and helped to brighten with their cheerfulness some of the dark hours that dragged by so slowly in our gloomy, filthy den.

I do not remember of hearing or seeing any religious service that winter in the prison, but there may have been such services held, and I did not see or hear them. But I am sure there must have been many a silent and earnest prayer wafted up to a merciful God, asking that His protecting arms might be thrown around us, and that we might soon be liberated from this accursed den, and once more be permitted to bask in the free, bright warm sunlight of heaven.

I remember one day of seeing one of the prisoners with quite a lot of cornbread in his arms start through the prison to sell or trade it to the prisoners. I do not know how he came to possess such a supply of bread, but it is quite likely he had stolen the meal from other prisoners; perhaps it was he who had stolen the meal from my mess. Be that as it may, there were others that looked on with suspicion, as well as myself, and they whispered the magic words: "Let's mug him." No sooner said than done. That corn-bread was scattered to the four winds, to be eagerly grabbed up by the half-famished men and greedily eaten.

Mr. Pedlar had sold out much more quickly than he expected to, but his profits were nit. If he stole the meal, they served him just right. He could not lay the blame on any certain one for his loss, for the boys butted into him from all directions, so he just had to grin and bear it.

This was one mode of "mugging," and the thieves and thugs in the prison practiced it on new prisoners that they thought had anything worth stealing. If anyone in the prison had money be could purchase from some of the best-natured guards sweet potatoes, cornbread, chickens and eggs. One dollar in greenbacks would buy as much as ten dollars in Confederate scrip.

There was a sutler in the prison part of the time that sold wheat bread and some few other notions, but there were very few of the prisoners had any money to buy anything with.

I noticed that those men that put on a bold front, kept up their courage and took what exercise they could each day seemed to hold their own a great deal better than those who, becoming discouraged, gave up hope at once; but I must admit that it requires a pretty stiff backbone, backed up by a double amount of nerve, for one to keep up his courage and cheerfulness where they are not only deprived of their liberty, but day after day and night after night are made to suffer with the cold for the want of clothing and fire, with hunger gnawing at their vitals. And then add to this suffering the creeping and crawling and biting of hundreds of vermin as they suck the life blood from the poor, emaciated bodies.

Surely one had to have nerves of steel and eyes of faith to see any silver lining behind as dark a cloud as this.

Small wonder then that under these distressing circumstances, with no ray of hope to lighten the gloom, that men would even court death by crossing the dead line, that the deadly bullet of the guard might put an end to their misery.

No commissioned officers were put in Cahaba prison with us privates, but among the batch of prisoners that arrived there in January was a Captain Hanchett. He was said to have belonged to the 16th Illinois Cavalry, and was Assistant Adjutant General to General Capron. He with about a dozen others had been captured by General Forest in Tennessee, and among them was an K. C. Spencer of the 8th Michigan Cavalry. Those two agreed to work together in an attempt to escape.

Captain Hanchett was in disguise, having traded his uniform for a citizen's suit after his capture, so was not known as an officer by the Confederates at Cahaba.

He had not been in the prison many days till he had matured a plan in his mind to release all the prisoners at Cahaba. His plan, as I have since learned, was as follows:

With a few trusty men to disarm the inside guards at night, rush out and capture the guards and arms outside of the stockade; then march to Selma some ten miles up the river, get arms, artillery and ammunition at the arsenal there, also horses; cross to the east side of the river on a ferry boat, and march to the Union lines at Pensacola, Florida, one hundred and fifty miles away.

If my memory serves me rightly, I think it was just before daylight, January 20th, 1865, the attempt was made to carry out this plan, but very few of the prisoners, perhaps twenty or twenty-five, knew anything about the contemplated outbreak.

So, like myself, when they were awakened by the slight confusion that was made by disarming the inner guard, they did not understand the matter.

The first words that I heard as I awoke was: "Damn you, steal another blanket, will you?" This was said by some of our men quite loud, so that the outside guards would think that the confusion was caused by the prisoners stealing from each other, and I heard one of the outside guards say: "Them damn Yankees are stealing blankets from one another again."

I raised up, and saw some of our men with guns on their shoulders. I then began to realize that there was trouble in the air and just then a voice called out loudly: "Fall in, one hundred men, quickly, to charge the outer gate!"

All was now confusion. I could hear the drums beating the long roll in the Confederate camps on the outside, while the leaders of the insurrection were calling for a hundred men to fall in. Other voices were calling just as loudly for all to lie down and keep quiet.

The consequence was that Captain Hanchett's grand plan to liberate the Cahaba prisoners was a failure. I understood at the time that they succeeded in disarming all the inner guards except one of those at the door; he made his escape, and it was he gave the alarm outside. Our men held the guard prisoners in the water closet. There was more or less confusion until just about daylight.

Colonel Jones plucked up courage to rush in his guards and one piece of artillery, and demanded that the guards and guns be surrendered within three minutes, or he would blow us all to hell.

In the meantime we were all crowded back in the south end of the building like a flock of sheep or hogs.

As there was a little delay in surrendering, Colonel Jones brought his guns to a ready, and his men had their fingers on their triggers, waiting the word to fire. But fortunately for us, the guards and guns were all returned at that moment, and Jones gave the order, "Recover arms," instead of "Fire."

General Henderson stated to me also that Colonel Jones had the two pieces of artillery loaded with canister that stood on the outside that morning, and was about to open fire on the prison, when he and a Confederate Lieutenant stepped in front of the pieces and told him not to fire, if he did he would kill them, and the Lieutenant called to the prisoners to bring out the captured guns, and also the guards, if they were alive. A prisoner answered him that the guards were unhurt, and were coming out as fast as they could through the crowd, and that the guns were also being brought out.

Finally, having got their guards and guns, Colonel Jones, with a great deal of bluster withdrew his men, closed the door and bolted it.

Reader, I will have to confess that my much-boasted courage and nerve deserted me for a short time that morning, especially at the moment those muskets were pointed at my head at the short range of ten feet.

I am pretty sure had those men got the command, "Fire!" this little story would never have been written by me.

In a short while the guards were brought in again, and we were all counted to see if any of us had got away during the night. Finding us all there, they then made a demand for us to give up the ring-leaders of the plot, and Colonel Jones said that not a damn bite would we get to eat until we did.

One of the guard told that he wounded one of the prisoners when they disarmed him, so then the prisoners were all ordered to strip to the skin and pass between two inspectors, holding our clothes above our heads that they might find the wounded man. One man was wounded slightly in the hand, but he passed through without being detected.

Then we were all passed through the lines again in the presence of the disarmed guard to see if they could identify any of those that disarmed them.

Two or three were identified and taken outside, and finally on the second day after the insurrection someone turned traitor and gave Captain Hanchett away, and he and his brave associates were taken out and placed in the dungeon.

On the third day after the attempted outbreak rations were issued to us again, and soon we all settled down to the same monotonous routine as before. I think it is just as well that the insurrection stopped where it did.

If we had succeeded in getting outside, there would have been numbers of us killed, and then it would have been impossible for us to have gotten away, for just at that time, General Henderson tells me, there were rumors that the Union General [James Harrison] Wilson was threatening Selma and Cahaba with his cavalry, and that the Confederates had sent heavy reinforcements to Selma, and of course they would have gobbled us all again, or killed us all.

I do not think it likely that Captain Hanchett was aware of this reinforcement, so had we escaped from the prison he would have marched us right into their hands again.

Poor, brave Captain Hanchett! It is said by those that knew him that when he saw his plan had failed that morning he cried like a child.

I think it would have been the better plan for him to have had a hundred men sworn to follow his lead, but I suppose he was afraid to let too many into his secret, for fear some of them would turn traitor and inform on him.

I have never been able to find out to a certainty his fate, but from the best information I can get, he was kept in the dungeon until we were all exchanged the following March, and then Colonel Jones took him out and put him in charge of two of his kindred spirits, and started toward Selma, with instructions to find some excuse to put him out of the way before they reached there, which they did before getting very far from Cahaba, and I think it more than likely that this is true, as Colonel Jones was just the kind of a man for that kind of dirty work.

General Henderson inquired of me if I knew what became of Hanchett, as he said he did not exchange him at Vicksburg while he was there, for he said he would have known him if he had.

If Colonel Jones had been such a man as Dr. Howard Henderson, we prisoners would have received better treatment. Jones deserved the same fate as Wirz of Andersonville fame did, but escaped it by sneaking out of the United States in disguise, but I am told he stole back in after years and located in New Orleans.

I was told that a Mrs. Gardiner, who lived near the prison, performed many acts of kindness, by passing through a hole in the stockade books and vegetables, but it was not my good fortune to learn of this in time to make use of the noble lady's charity.

There was also a Miss Marks, who was a kind nurse to the sick men outside in the hospitals. God will surely reward them for their unselfish kindness in those dark days. I trust I shall someday meet them in the sweet bye-and-bye.

After the insurrection our condition grew worse. Our guards were more strict, and the long dreary days and nights passed slowly by.

During the month of February it rained almost daily. The rebels told us that all the lowlands were flooded. Of course those heavy cold rains increased our suffering. Many got discouraged, sickened, and many died. No bright ray of hope penetrated through the dark clouds. Had our government abandoned us to our fate?

It began to look that way to us poor devils shut up in that filthy, lousy den, as we could not learn what was transpiring in the outside world.

I think it was about the last night in February. I was lying-asleep with the rest of my messmates, and gradually my mind drifted off into the land of dreams. I was in my old bedroom at my brother's, near College Hill, Ohio, looking out of the window Over Mr. Gray's peach orchard. The trees had the same beautiful green uniform tops that I had admired so much when I labored among them.

As I feasted my eyes on the delightful scene it slowly faded away and, presto, change! I am standing with my arms resting on the garden fence. There had been a gentle shower of rain, which made the young vegetables show their tiny heads from one end of the garden to the other, in their neat, straight rows.

No doubt my readers have times without number enjoyed looking at their own gardens just after a nice shower, when they had the same appearance as this garden had to me in my dream, and they can imagine how delighted I was with the pretty scene, it seemed so real to me, but, alas, I was rudely awakened to find I was still a prisoner in old Castle Morgan, and worse yet, my feet were just about to be engulfed by the muddy waters of the Alabama River, which had slyly crept into the prison whilst we slept.

Of course, as I was the longest man among my bed-fellows, it reached me first, and now the water kept rising until it covered the entire inside of our prison from two to three feet. This indeed seemed to add the cap sheaf to our misery.

No rest for any of us now; only those who were lucky enough to be in possession of a bunk. It was simply stand or wade around in the muddy waters. Like Noah's weary dove, there was no place for us to rest our feet.

Talk about the suffering in Andersonville, Saulsbury Castle, Thunder and Libby. Could it have been any more cruel than this? Some of our Sergeants had a talk with Colonel Jones, and pleaded with him to let the men march out upon dry land, but that heartless wretch answered: "No. Not as long as there is a damn Yankee's head above water can you come out of that stockade.'

Finally they shipped us a lot of cord-wood, with which platforms were built, on which we could climb and keep out of the water to some extent. There was no chance, of course, to cook our scant rations, so we ate them raw, washing them down with the filthy water that surrounded us.

They did send us in a few hardtacks that looked as though they were made out of bean meal, and they were as hard almost as flint rock.

I related my dream to my messmates, and told them that I believed this dream was a good omen, and so they all decided that it was a token of our speedy release.

As for myself, notwithstanding our gloomy surroundings, after this dream I felt encouraged, and thought I could discern a break in the dark clouds that so long had hidden us from the outside world.

Whether this was true or not, just about this time a notice was tacked up in our prison which said: "The latest dispatch from War

Department" was that there was to be a general exchange of prisoners man for man.

Oh! how the poor boys did yell and hollow when they read that note! Some thought the news was too good to be true, and others said the rebels only wanted to encourage us, and keep us from trying to make another break for liberty.

In a few days the water began to draw out of the prison, leaving some high points dry, on one of which Andrew Pouder, my bunkmate, and I made a fire out of some of the wood that had been brought in, and were sitting by it, warming ourselves. All at once the gates were opened, and a call was made for a boatload of prisoners to fall in for exchange.

At once Pouder and I fell into ranks, side by side, but being quite a distance from the gate, we were pretty well in the rear. The men kept passing out, and Pouder and I kept nearing the gate, and finally Pouder passed out and the gate was closed, shutting me in and Pouder out. I shall never forget the look that Pouder gave me as he saw the gate close between us, but he marched away, while I went back to the fire and sat down, feeling very lonely and desolate. r sat there brooding over my bad luck for quite a while, when

I heard the gate open again and, looking up, I saw Pouder and several others turned back into the prison. They had passed out more than they wanted.

FAREWELL TO CAHABA

There is an old saying that misery loves company, and it was true in my case. While there were plenty of comrades there, yet Pouder and I had been messmates all along, and a warm-attachment had sprung up between us, which bound us together like brothers, and while no doubt he was sorry to be turned back into that miserable den, and I shared this feeling with him to some extent, yet deep down within my heart I felt glad (God forgive me) to see him re-enter the gate and know we were still to have each other's companionship, let it be for weal or woe.

Pouder and I were now fortunate enough to get a good, dry bunk to sleep on, and we used it most of the day, passing the hours reading the New Testament, for I had a copy of the Scriptures during all my imprisonment, and read it over a number of times and found much comfort in it.

Finally the water gradually withdrew from the prison, and we could once more walk about without wading. It had performed one good act for us while it was there—it had drowned all the graybacks that it reached, and I know there must have been billions of them.

Pouder and I took off our old ragged clothes, a garment at a time, and held them over the fire until we roasted all the graybacks on them, and they would drop off into the fire, swell up and burst with a noise that would almost equal the popping of firecrackers, and the heat of the fire killed all the knits, so that we were entirely rid of the little pests, and could lay down now in our bunk at night and sleep peacefully.

And oh! what a sweet revenge it was to us to see those old graybacks that had been feasting for the last few months on our rich Yankee blood drop into the fire, burst and go up in smoke: We felt now we were even with one set of our enemies at least, but all earthly things, good or bad, must end sometime.

So on the morning of March 13, 1865, we were told our stay in old Cahaba prison was ended. The gates were thrown open and we all marched out and formed in two ranks in front of the prison, and

Colonel Jones made us a short speech, winding up by saying he hoped he would never see our faces back there again.

Jack Culp spoke up and said: "Colonel, we are tame Yanks now, but if we ever come back, we will be wild," but the Colonel did not see fit to make any reply to this thrust. And we were marched aboard a boat, and bidding a final good-bye to Cahaba, we were soon on our way, steaming up the river towards Selma.

No one but those that experienced it can tell with what thankful hearts we caught the last glimpse of the gloomy walls of old Cahaba, as we rounded a bend in the river a mile or so above it.

A fervent "Thank God" no doubt arose to the lips of many, who took that last look at that Hell on earth. Never while I live and keep my right mind can I forget the awful horrors of that den of misery.

In due time we arrived at Selma without accident and disembarked, and were marched into a stockade, to await transportation by rail. Next morning we were all rushed to the railroad station, with the understanding that a train would be there to take us on our way, but it turned out to be a mistake, so we were returned to the stockade.

On this little trip to the railroad and back my comrade Pouder and I had the good fortune to find two large plugs of tobacco, which we cut up into small pieces and traded the comrades for meal and meat, and by so doing we got a supply that lasted us until we reached the Union lines at the big, black river, besides keeping enough tobacco to do us through also, which was quite an item to us.

I suppose some of the guards lost the tobacco, or maybe some of our comrades. We heard no inquiries made about it.

It was here that the three-quart bucket was made to do duty, as Pouder and I made mush in it, and as we had plenty of meal we did not stint ourselves, you may be sure, but ate about all our stomachs would hold.

I am not positive, but I think we had to remain in Selma two nights. We were then put aboard a train and shipped to Jackson, Mississippi. I do not remember what route we went by, or what towns we passed through, but I think we passed one night in Meridian stockade. However, that does not matter.

We finally arrived at Jackson, and that was as far as the railroad 'was in running order. Here I spent my last Confederate money, paying five dollars to an old colored "auntie" for a chicken pie, and Pouder and I ate it and pronounced it the best chicken pie we ever ate. It certainly was more toothsome than cornbread made from meal that had been ground, cob and all, and sometimes a little musty at that.

Some of us drew a few new clothes at Jackson that had been forwarded by the government that far for our use. All that I remember of getting was a pair of socks. Or I may have gotten a cap, as I remember of losing my head covering somewhere on the trip, and I do not remember how I did manage until I got to parole camp.

From Jackson to the big, black river we had to foot it, and as the distance was forty miles, it took us two days to make the trip. The first day the weather was nice; the roads were in good condition, and we got along fine, making very good time for men in our condition. I assure you we had no surplus flesh to carry. The second day it set in to rain, and soon the roads became muddy and slippery, and our old, ragged clothing became thoroughly wet through, and this made it everything else but pleasant for us.

My old shoes were so worn that they became an encumbrance to me, so I cast them aside and marched in my sock feet.

I had said to Comrade Pouder that second morning that if any of us reached the big, black river that night, that I was going to be one among them, so I waded along through the mud, trying hard to keep up my courage, though I must say the rain rather dampened it, and the muddy roads clogged it, but freedom was on the other side of the big Black.

So I took a fresh chew of tobacco and forged ahead. Ah! here comes one of our escort, riding back from the front. What can he want back here? Listen, he is speaking:

"Gentlemen," he says, "it's the commanding officer's wishes that you keep well closed up, if you please, as he does not want any straggling."

Well, what do you think of that? He calls us gentlemen! Really, that almost took my breath away.

We must be nearing God's country, and this cavalryman already is beginning to be influenced by it, but come to think of it, he made no mistake in calling us gentlemen, for we were a very gentle crowd just then.

I think it is very likely that there were men on this trip that gave out, but as I was pretty well toward the front, I do not know what was taking place in the rear. I do not know who our escort was or what the officer's name was that was in command, but from what I saw and heard, all the prisoners were treated humanely on this trip.

When we drew rations and started, some of the boys asked the commander how long those rations were to do us, and he answered: "Until we reach some place where I can draw more," and he kept his word. Wherever he could draw rations, he did so. By this means we fared very well on the trip; better, I think, than we would had Jones brought us through.

It continued to rain until our advance reached the river about sundown. I had made my word good—I was there among them, though my limbs were so stiff and sore I could barely lift my feet clear of the ground, and I had to move them with a kind of sliding motion.

Comrade Pouder was also among the lucky numbers to arrive there in the advance. Yes, we had reached the Rubicon, but it was so late in the evening those in charge of affairs there desired us to wait till morning before allowing us to cross over.

They wished us to go back about a quarter of a mile and camp for the night. This did not please us prisoners a little bit, and it took some strong arguments by both Yankees and rebels to persuade us to turn back, but our officers promised to send us over rations that night.

So finally we reluctantly turned back, and went into camp in an old deadening, where there was an abundance of wood. Pouder and I took possession of a huge log heap, and waiting until nearly all had got their fires going before kindling ours, then we had a glorious fire all to ourselves.

The rain having now ceased, we soon had our old rags nice and dry, and taking our good friend, the three-quart bucket, we hunted up some water and soon had it full of steaming hot mush.

I think if I mistake not that Comrade Pouder and I got on the outside of six quarts of mush that night; then, spreading out our old rags, we lay our tired bodies down to rest.

Directly after lying down we heard our fellows calling, "Come and get your rations," but as our stomachs were already full of mush we closed our eyes and were soon in the land of dreams.

The next morning we awoke feeling very much refreshed. The sky was cloudless and the beautiful sun arose bright and warm. Pouder and I arose with it, and bringing forth our three-quart bucket, we soon had our breakfast mush cooked, and, sitting down, we partook of our last meal under the Stars and Bars—none too soon either, as our meal had begun to get musty from getting damp the day before. ,

Breakfast eaten, we fell into ranks, and once more made our way to the river, where the officers were soon busy calling the roll, and. as fast as we answered to our names, we passed over the pontoon bridge to freedom, into Gods country, under the bright folds of Old Glory, where we yelled and shouted ourselves hoarse with thankfulness and joy.

We were halted here a short while to await a train from Vicksburg, which soon appeared, and we were hustled aboard and taken to parole camp four miles back of Vicksburg, where we arrived March 21st, 1865.

On the train that brought us here were some colored soldiers as train guards, and as they were the first colored soldiers I had ever seen, they were quite a curiosity to me, and interested me very much.

At the camp we found others. They were dressed neatly, wore white gloves, and took great pride in their various duties.

Here we were organized into companies and battalions, and the companies were divided into messes of ten.

Comrade Pouder and I were assigned to Company 'C," 3rd Battalion.

We drew tents, blankets, clothing and a full supply of rations. At first some heartless commissary, thinking we were so near starved we would eat any old thing, issued us some stale, wormy hardtack, but we soon gave them to understand that that kind of business had to be cut out at once, and after that our rations were all right. The hardtack we got was equal to soda crackers.

Sergeants had charge of battalions and Corporals had charge of companies and messes; I had charge of one mess that was supposed to contain ten men, but in reality there were only eight at the beginning and one of these was taken sick and sent to the hospital, but still they gave me rations for ten men. So my mess fared sumptuously every day.

We had no duty to perform but to keep ourselves and quarters neat and clean, and cook and eat, so we soon began to fill out and look like men once more.

And here I wish to say that while we were on the way here from prison we met quite a large number of Confederates who had been exchanged, and were on the way home. There was a remarkable contrast between us.

We were lean, ragged and dirty and carried a little old cornmeal, tied up perhaps in a little old dirty rag, while they looked well fed, were clean and comfortably clothed; had haversacks that were well filled with crackers, coffee, sugar and meat. This I will vouch for, as some of them kindly shared their rations with us.

The next day after arriving at parole camp, I sent the following letter to my people at home:

"Parole Camp in rear of Vicksburg, Mississippi,

March 22nd, 1865.

"Dear Parents, Brothers and Sisters:

"It is with feelings of deep gratitude I seat myself this beautiful day to inform you of my present whereabouts, and also of my good health, although for the past few months I have had some of the roughest experiences that I ever had. But thanks be to God for His mercy, who has graciously spared my life through many dangers that were seen, as well perhaps from many that were not seen, by His poor,' unprofitable servant.

"Yes, I have passed safely through many dangers, privations and hardships, and was brought through the rough lines yesterday at the Big Black River, and am at present pleasantly situated in parole camp, four miles in rear of Vicksburg, Mississippi.

"I shall not attempt at this time to describe to you all the various scenes that I have passed through, but will do that sometime in future, when I have better accommodations for writing than I have at present.

"All I wish to do at this is to let you know I have got back to God's country alive and well, and I hope I may never be caught in another such a scrape.

"I will simply say this: I was captured by the enemy at Franklin, Tennessee, on the 30th of last November and marched from there to Cherokee Station, Alabama, where we boarded the cars and were shipped to Meridian, Mississippi, where we remained in a stockade about one month.

"We were then shipped by rail to Selma, Alabama, and then took it afoot, ten miles further, to Cahaba, and placed in Castle Morgan, where we were kept till the 13th of March, when we left there on parole for our lines, where we arrived yesterday, and were received into camp under the starry folds, of our glorious old flag.

"I suppose a happier set of men was never seen than we were when we stepped inside our lines. My heart swelled with thankfulness to the Heavenly Father for this great deliverance from our enemies.

"I suppose you have been in great trouble about me since I was captured, but now you may let your mind rest easy, for I am all right, and I hope and pray you are all alive and well at home, for I have not heard a word from any of you since my capture.

"I wrote you two letters while in prison, but do not know whether you received them or not. Write me as soon as you receive this, and tell me all the news.

"I would love to know where the 50th is and how many were killed and wounded at Franklin.

"The Christian Sanitary Commission are here, doing all in their power to make us comfortable and happy. May God bless them in their noble work.

"I have many things to tell you, but will have to pass them by for this time.

"Direct Company "C," 3rd Battalion, Parole Camp, rear Vicksburg, Mississippi.

"I cannot tell you anything of future movements. Andrew Pouder is with me, well and hardy. My love and best wishes to one and all.

"From your loving son and brother,

"Erastus Winters."

I had not been in camp here but a few days until I received two letters from some of my sisters at home, but they had been written for some time, as they were held at Vicksburg to await our arrival; but nevertheless I was certainly glad to get them and hear from home once more, if they were a little old.

Comrade Pouder and I got a pass one day and went up to visit Vicksburg. We neither of us had any money, but I had the good fortune while there to find a fifty-cent shin plaster lying in the gutter. It had been so long since I had any money I came near not recognizing it as money. We made use of it, but I have forgotten what we purchased with it.

We spent a good portion of the day looking around over the Bluff City, but I have no remembrance now of anything we saw, so I judge we saw nothing that made any very lasting impressions on my mind.

On March 29th I sent the following letter home to my parents:

"Camp Fisk, four miles south of Vicksburg,

"March 29th, 1865.

"My Dear Parents, Brothers and Sisters;

"Once more am I permitted the pleasure of seating myself to write you all a short letter to inform you all of my present good health and prosperity.

"I have just received two letters, one from sister Phebe and one from sister Lucretia. They have been written for some time, but yet they were new to me, and I was glad to hear you were all living and in health when they were written.

"But oh! how sorry I was to hear of the death of Lieutenant Pine. I don't know what will become of Company 'K' now. I have not heard anything from the regiment yet, but I expect a great many of my comrades met their death at Franklin and Nashville.

"I am thankful that a kind and watchful Heavenly Father has spared my life thus far, though surrounded by many dangers and exposed to many hardships.

"First, I was threatened with death from powder and ball; second, was nearly frozen to death; third, was nearly marched to death; fourth, was nearly starved to death; and fifthly, was kept in prison nearly a week with the water standing knee deep over the entire inside of the prison; yet out of all these dangers, trials and tribulations the good Lord delivered me. All honor, thanksgiving and praise be to His name.

"I will give just a short sketch of my experience since the 30th of last November:

"I was captured by the enemy that day at Franklin with sixty-two others of my regiment, and taken back to Columbia and kept in an old fort there until the 14th of December, and although the weather was very cold, we got barely enough wood to cook our little cornmeal they gave us.

"All I had to protect me from the cold was a small part of a blanket that I gathered up somewhere on the route. But many of the poor boys were not that well off.

"If a prisoner had a good blanket or overcoat, the rebs would take it and leave him with nothing to screen him from the cold winds and storms that we were compelled to lay out in.

"Leaving Columbia the 14th of December, we marched to Cherokee, Alabama. This was the worst march I ever experienced. The mud and slush were shoe mouth deep, beside the rain and snow that we had to battle with. We were eight days on this trip. We drew a little cornmeal and a little poor beef each day, until we reached Cherokee, where we were given a few hardtacks, put aboard platform cars and shipped to Corinth, Mississippi. The weather meantime was very cold, and we suffered a great deal from the exposure in riding in the night on open cars.

"We arrived here on the morning of the 23rd; remained here till next day, boarded the cars again, and were sent to Meridian, Mississippi, arriving there on Christmas night, having passed our Christmas on the cars, and our dinner was raw corn, of which there was plenty at all the stations on the road.

"Here we were placed in a stockade and kept until the 8th of January, 1865. We did not fare so badly here. A quart of meal, a few nigger peas, a little beef, pork or spareribs for a day's ration to each man. And having got hold of some Confederate money, I bought some sweet potatoes. They were plentiful here. We had some very good eating.

"But on the 9th of January we were once more placed aboard the cars and shipped to Cahaba, Alabama, arriving there on the 12th. Here our misery began in dead earnest. There were something over three thousand prisoners confined here. These were divided into companies of one hundred men each, and these again divided into messes of ten men each, and each mess drew a large bake oven.

"Once every ten days one man would be passed out after wood, and what he could carry in at one trip would have to run us for cooking purposes for ten days. The wood was mostly green, and there was so much smoke in our crowded cook-yard that some of the men were almost blinded with it.

"We did not get half enough to eat, and what we did get we had to eat half cooked for the want of wood.

"The prison was overcrowded with men. We could not sit or stand anywhere without someone crowding against us, except when lying down at night, trying to sleep; and then we could not rest, for the place was simply alive with body lice—graybacks, we called them.

"One morning before daylight, just before we were exchanged, a few ringleaders among the prisoners made an attempt to liberate us all.

They disarmed all the inner guard except one; he made his escape to the outside, and gave the alarm, and the plan proved a failure.

"It was three days before they found out the leaders of the insurrection, and we never got a bite to eat during that time.

"About six hundred of the men had bunks to sleep on, but the balance of us had to sleep on the ground. All through February it rained almost daily, and about two weeks before we came out the water from the Alabama River came in and covered the entire inside of the prison from two to three feet.

"Fortunately for us, a boat load was taken out for exchange at this time, and that gave the remainder of us a chance to occupy the bunks, and keep out of the water.

"Finally, on the 13th of March, we were all taken out, and furnished transportation as fair as Jackson, Mississippi.

"Then after a two days' march, we were received into our lines at the Big Black River on the 20th or 21st of March.

"This is only an outline sketch. I will fill it up with particulars when I reach home.

"We are now pleasantly situated at four mile bridge back of Vicksburg. We have good quarters to stay in; get plenty to eat; have drawn new clothing, and we begin to feel like men once more.

"I wrote you a few lines the next day after my arrival here, and I suppose you have received it by this time.

"I am at present in good health, and of course, in good spirits again.

"Write to me soon, and tell me all the news, both good and bad.

"Direct to camp Fisk, near Vicksburg, Mississippi, Company "C", Third Battalion, ex-prisoners of war.

"Give my love and best wishes to all inquiring friends, and don't forget to choose a large portion for yourselves.

"I am as ever, your loving son and brother, who wishes the choicest blessings of Heaven to rest upon you all.

"Erastus Winters."

DEATH OF PRESIDENT LINCOLN

One day while here there arrived a lot of men from Andersonville prison. Poor boys! what a sad plight they were in; many of them so weak and emaciated we had to dead them from the cars to

How could men lose all feelings of humanity, so as to treat their fellow beings as our prisoners were treated in the Southern prisons, during the War of the Rebellion?

Surely if there is a place of future punishment, and the Bible teaches me there is, and I believe it with all my heart, then those who were the cause of so much suffering and death in those awful days, will someday receive their just reward in full measure, shaken down and running over.

Henry Wirz, commander at Andersonville, was tried and hung after the war.—Ed. 2017

I have no hard feelings against the Confederate soldier, who met us face to face on the field of battle, and fought us bravely for what he thought was right. I can meet the old gray-headed veteran now who wore the grey, and grasp him by the hand without a thought of bitterness or malice or hatred in my heart, but never while I live can I forget the treatment we received from their leaders in those cruel, deadly dens in the South.

We were here in camp yet when the word reached us that our beloved President Abraham Lincoln's life had been snuffed out by the cruel hand of an assassin. This cast a gloom over our cheerful camp, and mutterings for a speedy revenge for the cruel act were heard on all sides.

Oh! why did they not let that broken-hearted man live to finish the work he had been successfully engaged in since 1861?

Sad to think that just as the dark clouds of war began to roll by, the grand and noble Lincoln, with malice towards none, but with charity for all, should die by the hand of a murderous assassin. It is hard to realize why he should have been cut down, just as peace was almost within his sight.

The Confederate Commissioner of Exchange, Colonel Henderson (or rather General as he tells me; he had now been promoted to Brigadier General), was in Vicksburg when the news came that the President had been murdered. Excitement ran high, and it was feared that the colored soldiers would kill General Henderson, on sight, knowing him to be a Confederate. Our officers saw to having him put aboard a light engine and run out to the Big Black River, and set across into the Confederate lines.

General Henderson says that was about the wildest ride he ever made, and he was jolted so he could scarcely keep his seat; the road was rough, the engineer badly scared, and he threw the throttle wide open and let her pound.

I heard the engine pass our camp that night, but did not know until afterward what her errand was.

The Confederate Texas Cavalry were on duty at the Big Black River, and Henderson says when he told them of the murder of Lincoln, that as tough and hard as those Texans have the reputation of being, that a number of them shed tears, and well they might, for they had lost a true friend.

In a few days matters quieted down, and General Henderson came back to Vicksburg to attend to his duties.

We remained here in this camp about one month; that is, I speak of those that I came from Cahaba with. There were others that were before us, and there were others that came afterward.

Everything went along smoothly except our water supply made several of the men sick.

The soil there was a black loam and there was no limestone in it, hence the water was not very good for health.

I think, perhaps, it was either the 23rd or 24th of April that we finally broke camp, and went to Vicksburg.

I cannot now remember whether we marched or went by rail; however, that doesn't matter. I know we got there by some means, and from the best information I can gather, some twenty-three hundred of us were put aboard the steamer *Sultana*; there were some cabin passengers, and among them I am told were nine ladies. There was also a company of soldiers put aboard.

The *Sultana* was a side-wheeled boat, and a pretty large sized steamer, but the reader can see at once she was overloaded, but graft, dear reader, was practiced in those days just the same as now.

And while there were other boats lying at Vicksburg that would have been glad to have had a part of us for a cargo, as Uncle Sam was paying so much a head to have us shipped north at that time, yet by some hocus pocus between the officers of the *Sultana* and the transportation officers, in which money played the chief part, we were all crowded aboard the one boat, something like a flock of sheep or a drove of hogs.

But we prisoners, at least those of us from Cahaba, were used to being crowded, and therefore we did not pay much attention to being crowded on board the boat, and then our minds were filled up with thoughts of home, and the loved ones awaiting us there.

Here were men that had been in prison from four months to two years; had suffered from cold, hunger, disease and exposure of all kinds, and their poor, weak bodies had been preyed upon by vermin. But now for the time being, all these things were forgotten. We were on our way home, and this took full possession of our minds, crowding out all thoughts of danger, disaster or suffering.

We were a merry-hearted, jolly set of men and boys as the *Sultana* was turned loose from the wharf at Vicksburg, swung out into midstream, and turned her prow toward the North with her living freight of human beings.

Everything as far as we could see was running smoothly, as the overloaded Sultana plowed her way slowly onward through the muddy waters of the Mississippi.

At [Helena, Arkansas, a photographer by some good fortune took a picture of the boat](), showing her overloaded condition while she was lying at the wharf, and a number of those photographs are yet in existence throughout the country.

But very few of us thought or dreamed of danger, but whiled away the time gazing at the shifting scenes along the shore, playing little tricks on each other, singing little songs, telling little jokes; laughing and talking about the happy times we expected to have when we reached our homes in receiving the warm and welcome caresses of fathers, mothers, brothers, sisters, wives, sweethearts and friends.

Reader, put yourself in our place, and then you may begin to realize what a happy lot we were. Such was the condition of the men and boys on board the Steamer *Sultana*, when she steamed up to the wharf at Memphis, Tennessee, in the evening of April 26th, 1865.

We lay here for some time while the boat hands were unloading a lot of sugar that had been stored in the hold. Some of the ex-prisoners helped unload the sugar; I believe they were paid by the hour for their work.

By some means one of the hogsheads of sugar was bursted and a number of the men and boys had quite a picnic eating sugar, and carrying off more for future use.

Comrade Pouder was one among the number; besides bringing up all we wanted to eat at that time, he filled our ever-ready three-quart bucket, with the expectation of having it for future use, but alas! it was not so ordered. And as this is perhaps the last time I will have occasion to mention our good friend, we may as well take our leave of it here, for it went down in the wreck a few hours after being filled with sweetness. And its remains for aught I know are resting today on the slimy bottom of the Mississippi.

Farewell, old friend, your mission is ended; we shall always remember with pleasure the true and faithful service you rendered us in cruel Cahaba, and although you finally went down to a watery grave, and we missed you sorely, yet as we call to mind how you appeared to us as we fondly gazed on you for the last time, our thoughts of thee are very sweet.

I now approach a period in these reminiscences that I fain would forget and pass by, but I believe I said back near the beginning that I intended to tell all the snaps and snarls I got into, good or bad, so if I would jump over what now happened I would not be treating my readers fair, neither would I be fulfilling my agreement.

So that no matter how hard and disagreeable the task may be, I feel under obligations to make the attempt, though I know that after I have done the best I can to describe the awful scene, that the half will not be told.

We did not leave the wharf at Memphis until after midnight, so it was the morning of April 27th when we left there and steamed across the river to a coal barge or barges, and stopped to take on coal.

All of us had sought some place of repose, while we were stopping at Memphis, and every available foot of space was occupied by the men from the boiler deck to the hurricane roof, and after we had lain down, it was simply impossible for a person to walk over the boat anywhere without stepping on someone.

Comrade Pouder of Company "K," Comrade John Fox, Corporal, Company "A," and Comrade M. L. Rice, Private, Company "A" and myself, all of the 50th Ohio, bunked together, and chose a spot just forward of the smokestacks on the cabin deck.

From the best information I have been able to get, it was about two o'clock in the morning, when the *Sultana* swung loose from the coal barges to resume her journey up the river. At that drowsy time in the early morning, it can be taken for granted that the majority of us were sleeping peacefully, dreaming of the old home, and the joys awaiting us there.

It was nearing the hour of three, and the *Sultana* had reached a point some eight or ten miles above Memphis at the head of the Island called, "The Old Hen and Chickens."

No danger was anticipated, and without any warning being given, all at once a terrific crash occurred; one of the boilers had given way with a noise those who chanced to be awake said, resembled the discharge of a battery of artillery.

The noise of the explosion added to the slight scalds and burns I received awoke me, and I uttered the exclamation, "Oh!" as I found myself slipping down an incline, and landed on my feet on the coal pile in front of the furnaces.

I knew something terrible had happened, but did not for a few moments realize just what it was. The steam was so stifling, I could scarcely breathe where I was, so I carefully treaded my way out onto the bow of the boat, and soon learned what had happened. I saw nothing of the three comrades I had been sleeping with. All was confusion. Pandemonium reigned supreme.

Wounded men, and men who were pinioned down with iron and timbers were screaming and begging for help, men were crying, men were praying, and men were cursing and swearing; men were walking about wringing their hands and crying out, "What shall I do?" Others stood as if dazed. Some of the men had been killed while they slept, and never knew what happened. Others awoke to find themselves adrift in the chilly waters of the Mississippi.

The boat took fire immediately, and as it lit up the scene I could see that the surrounding water was rapidly being filled up with a struggling mass of men, that were now jumping overboard to escape the fast increasing flames.

It was just at this time, my attention was attracted to some men who were trying to launch a large stage plank, and also to the voice of someone, who was saying, "You men that can't swim better follow this plank." That appealed to me, for I knew no more about swimming than a year-old child, so I took hold, and helped shove the plank overboard, and jumped after it.

The plank shot down under the water, but soon came to the surface, and righted itself with just as many men on it and around it, as was possible to get near it.

I was one among the number that thought the only place of safety for me was on top of that plank. We only drifted a short distance till the plank was turned completely over. I was not looking for anything of that kind to happen, and taken off my guard, I lost my hold on the plank, and sunk beneath the waters.

And now once more in my life, I had reached a point where my boasted courage and nerve forsook me. I knew I could not swim, and thinking I would never reach that plank again, all thoughts of being saved left me, and for a few brief moments, while I was under the water, I lost hope and the thought flashed through my mind that this was the end, and that the time had come when I must yield up my life.

But what is this that my head has come in contact with? I reach out my hand, and grasp it. Thank God, it's that blessed old stage plank. My courage revives, hope once more fills my breast; I place my trust in my Heavenly Father, and by his mercy, and through his power, I will yet reach a place of safety. I struggle on, I lose hope no more; I become more rational, and act with more deliberation. I beg my comrades to be more quiet and though the plank was turned over a number of times, I always managed to retain my hold on it. But every time it would turn over a number would be washed off who would never reach it again.

Another comrade, whom I think from what I have learned since must have been Comrade Henry Gambill of Company "B," 14th Kentucky Infantry was on the plank, and acted very cool. He and I helped another comrade on the plank two or three times, but I think the poor fellow was finally washed off and lost.

We drifted on out of the mass of men around the wreck until we reached dead water, and by this time, there was only about six of us left on the plank, and perhaps not more than four or five.

The river was very high, and all the lowlands were under water at the time. I got hold of a piece of weatherboard that was floating, and standing upon the plank, began to paddle toward a mass of driftwood that was stationary that I could see a short distance in front of us, for now the first streaks of daylight began to show in the east, and we could begin to see our surroundings.

The stern end of our plank, I may call it, caught on a young cotton wood bush, and we could have remained there and been rescued, but I was not satisfied to stay there.

I saw a pole or dead sapling floating in the water that I managed to get hold of. It was about fifteen feet in length and had a crooked root on it. Taking this in my hands, I walked forward to the bow of the plank as close as I dared and reached for that drift pile, and by good fortune my pole would reach it, and making my pole fast by hooking it over some of the trash, I pulled the plank loose from the bush and brought it up to the drift pile, onto which I stepped, and felt I was saved.

By this time it was fairly daylight and some comrades that had escaped to an old stable that was surrounded by water saw us, and they called to us and said we could wade the water anywhere there, and getting down and trying it, I found it about waist deep, and selfishly leaving my comrades on the plank, I waded to the old building, and climbing up I sat down beside the comrades already there.

And the four or five comrades I left with the plank worked it to the side of the building, and got up with us. There was no roof on the building, and we roosted up there like birds waiting to be rescued.

While making our perilous trip on the plank in the early hours of the morning, I had heard a comrade on the plank praying, if it could be called a prayer. He addressed the Heavenly Father, and rehearsed to Him all the trials, privations and hardships that we had endured, and how we had finally started for our homes with our hearts filled with joyful anticipations of the pleasures we expected to enjoy with our friends and loved ones when we would reach there, and now for this last disaster to overtake us.

He prayed earnestly if God would only spare his life to reach his home, he would devote the balance of his days to His service. But at the time, I had not recognized the voice, but now as daylight had come, I looked around me to see who had been saved with me, and I found that it was Corporal John Fox that had been praying, and one of the comrades I had been sleeping with when the explosion occurred.

Comrade Fox after getting on the building with us, drew from his pocket a plug of tobacco that was considerably swollen, having come in contact with the water in the river.

Fox passed his tobacco around among us, and after a few jokes about its swollen condition, we each took a chew, and had quite a sociable time chewing it.

It seems that when the boiler exploded, it blew a hole right up through the cabin deck and the hurricane deck, forming a large crater; those on the hurricane roof that were not blown into the river at the time, could look down into the crater, and see the fire as it kindled up at the bottom, and merciful God! what a scene that was to look at; they could see as the fire lit up the interior of the crater, dead men, crippled men; men fastened down with iron and timbers, and all those had to remain down in there and burn up, as there was no help for them. That was one scene I was mercifully spared the pain of gazing on.

Fortunately, I happened to be lying near the outer edge of the crater, and came down outside of where the fire started, and was not struck with any flying timbers or iron, and did not remain on the boat long enough after the explosion to witness some of the horrible scenes that others did. But God knows I saw enough and more than I ever wish to see again.

When we drifted away from the wreck on that plank, all we could see as far as the fire lit up, the dark river was a struggling mass of human heads. It looked at times as though hundreds would catch hold of each other at once, and sink down to Eternity together; two or three men, perhaps, would quarrel and fight over the possession of a plank that with proper care would have saved them all, until they would all sink down to a watery grave.

Many good swimmers were lost by drowning; men catching them, and pulling them under. There are no words in the English language that can fully and fittingly describe the horrible and heartrending scenes that we survivors were eye witnesses of that morning.

No artist, I care not how clever he may be with his brush, can paint a picture as full of horrors as the picture that was painted on my memory, that April morning, 1865.

And though forty years have passed by since then, the picture has never faded, but stands out in bold relief on the canvass of memory today, showing all the cruel details as plainly as it did that never-to-be-forgotten morning.

Many of the men were scalded from the crown of their heads to the soles of their feet; a number were crippled by the explosion, so that it was impossible for them to be saved, and they begged their comrades to throw them overboard, and let them drown instead of burning to death, and this was done when all hope of having them was gone, and the poor victims thanked those whose-hard lot it was to perform this heartrending task.

Out of the ten or twelve ladies that were aboard, not more than three of four were rescued.

The official report of the lives lost at the time was near sixteen hundred, and as quite a number died after being taken to the hospitals, no doubt the loss was fully sixteen hundred if not more.

It is still the worst maritime disaster in United States history. The most recent evidence indicates more than 1,700 died, almost 200 higher than the 1,512 deaths attributed to the Titanic. The main channel of the Mississippi now flows about 2 miles (3 km) east of its 1865 position and in 1982, archaeologists found what they believe are remnants of the Sultana under a soybean field. —Ed. 2017

INCIDENTS IN THE HOSPITAL

Some twenty-five or thirty comrades clung to the old wreck until she had burned to the water's edge, and by this time she had drifted near shore. So the comrades managed to make a raft of the broken and fire-scorched timbers, on which they finally reached the shore in safety, just as the old hull sank to the bottom, throwing up a cloud of steam and water to a height of several feet into the air.

Such was the story that Comrade Jack Culp of my Company, who was one of those rescued on the raft, related to me, and his story agrees with that told by Comrade Samuel J. Thrasher of Company "G" 6th Kentucky in a book called, *The Loss of the Sultana*, published by the survivors several years ago.

I have never forgotten the agonizing cries for help I heard that morning. It seems after the lapse of forty years, I can still hear the pleadings of the poor boys, as they clung to the trees and bushes along the shores, and on the islands. Many of them died after reaching a place of safety. The remains of hundreds of them were never found. Their bones lie scattered from where the explosion occurred to the Gulf.

Surely the Government ought to erect and dedicate a monument to their memory, for they are worthy. They not only fought for this Government, but they died for it. When suffering from cold, hunger, vermin and other inhuman treatment, and a promise was held out to them of better conditions if they would renounce their Government, they rejected the offer with scorn, and proved true to their flag, and yielded up their lives in its service. Yet strange to relate, they are not even mentioned in history.

There are hundreds of people in this country today that are well posted in history, yet don't know there ever was a boat named "The Sultana"; much less do they know that her destruction caused the loss of sixteen hundred brave boys who wore the blue in defense of the very flag that now protects them.

It's an outrage and a shame that those brave boys and true, who gave their best days in defense of this Government, and finally died a cruel death before reaching home, should be ignored and forgotten by those whose delight it ought to be to do them honor.

A year ago, one of the leading papers of Cincinnati published a list of the marine disasters since 1841, involving great loss of life. Was the *Sultana* mentioned in that list? No, indeed, I suppose the publisher had never heard or read of such a boat. When the *Maine* was blown up [in Havana Harbor, February 15, 1898] in twenty-four hours it was known all over the world and today there is scarcely a school boy or girl but what can tell you something about the *Maine*. Just so it is in regard to the *General Slocum* that burnt, loaded with school children, and just so it will be with the U. S. Gunboat *Bennington* which blew up a few days ago [July 21, 1905] in San Diego, California, causing the loss of perhaps one hundred lives. All these of course are appalling disasters, but the *Sultana* which towers above them all with her loss of sixteen hundred lives is not once mentioned in history only in the little book that the survivors themselves published a few years ago. Some try to whitewash this over by saying that so many things of vital interest had taken place at this time that it had simply been overlooked. The President had been murdered, a four years' war was just coming to a close and peace was in sight. 'Well, certainly those were very interesting events, but I am sorry that the writers of history thought that the burning and drowning of sixteen hundred poor ex-prisoners of war a matter too insignificant to bring before the minds of their readers.

I trust that someone who can get Congress interested in this matter, will bring the subject before them, and be successful in getting a monument erected in memory of those poor boys, who lost their lives battling with the cruel waves of the Father of Waters; whose remains never received a decent burial, because they were never found.

But please excuse me, reader. I was about to leave myself stranded on the old stable chewing tobacco. Those of us who had found a refuge on the old building remained there until perhaps 9 or 10 o'clock in the morning before we were taken off. We were kept busy fighting the buffalo gnats, as they came around us in swarms. Some of us were not very well blessed with clothing just at that time, and those gnats had a fair show to get in their work, and they were not slow to improve their opportunity.

None of us in that crowd would have been very presentable in my ladies drawing room; as for myself, my dress suit at that time consisted of blouse shirt, drawers and one sock. Many of my comrades were not even that well blessed.

My pants had got water soaked, and were in my way, and I had discarded them while in the river. Many others had stripped off all their clothing, in order that they might not impede them while swimming; hence they were entirely nude when rescued. While seated up there on the old building, we could see several comrades clinging to bushes and trees up and down the shore, and while they were in a manner safe, yet they kept hollowing for help.

I am not positive, but I think this was on the Arkansas side of the river, where we were stranded. Finally, a boat steamed in as close to us as she could, and then sent the yawl, and took us off our roost. I do not remember the name of the boat, but I do remember the first object that I ran up against as I stepped aboard the boat, was a large size glass of whiskey. Now I had never been a lover of whiskey, nor am I at present, but at that moment I was chilled through and through, and as you may expect under these circumstances, it did not require any coaxing for me to speedily place myself outside that whiskey, and I am sure it did me no harm, but soon warmed me up, though a cup of strong coffee perhaps would have answered the same purpose.

I walked on into the dining room, and seating myself at the table, I partook of a good warm breakfast of hot coffee, fried sweet potatoes, biscuits, butter and other good things too tedious to mention.

Plenty of whisky was setting around over the boat, but I did not indulge in any more; that one glass fixed me up in good shape. By the time I had finished eating my breakfast, the boat had reached the wharf at Memphis. A newspaper reporter met me, took my name and regiment, saying his would be the first news of the disaster that would reach the Cincinnati papers.

At the wharf, the Christian Commission people met us, and did what they could for our comfort, furnishing each one as far as possible with dry undergarments.

I was furnished a pair of drawers, placed in an ambulance, and taken to Adams' general hospital No. 3. Here I was furnished dry hospital clothes, and given a cot, of which I took possession, and lay down to rest and study over the appalling scenes that I had been an eye-witness of that morning.

I was slightly scalded on face, neck, hands, feet and left arm; others were scalded so much worse than I, and there was such a number of them, they did not come to dress my wounds until nearly night, and my wounds became very dry and felt very unpleasant, and I still remember how cool and nice they felt after they had been dressed.

I rested very well that night; the next day I was scarcely able to move; every muscle in my body was sore. I felt as though someone had beaten me all over the body with a club. This was caused by the exertion I made in the river, and by the shaking up I got at the time of the explosion.

I never have seen Comrade Fox since parting with him on the rescue boat, but I trust he arrived home safe, and that he kept his promise faithfully that he made to his Heavenly Father that morning, on that blessed old *Sultana* stage plank while hundreds of his comrades were perishing around him.

Comrade Rice I never saw or heard of after the explosion, so must number him among the lost. He was a good, clever boy, and was the only one among us four comrades that bunked together on the *Sultana* that had any money. He had received money from home while lying in parole camp back of Vicksburg. He was generous with it; he bought some knickknacks, and shared them with his comrades on the boat on the way to Memphis.

Of we four comrades sleeping together on the *Sultana* three were rescued—namely, Pouder, Fox and myself.

As I was lying on my cot, the next day after the explosion, I heard one of the doors open at the far end of the ward. I looked up, and who should I see enter but my old chum and messmate, Comrade Pouder. He saw me the instant I saw him, and came to me, his face wreathed in smiles. We were certainly glad to meet and greet each other again after our rude parting on board the *Sultana*.

We related to each other our experience, and how we were rescued, and then he bade me good-bye as he told me all who were able to travel were to be shipped north to Columbus, Ohio, that afternoon, so I met him no more until I reached home, and paid him a visit.

Comrade Pouder is still living at this date, July 26, 1905. He resides with his wife at Liberty, Union County, Indiana. He and I have always managed to keep in touch with each other by corresponding and visiting with each other.

It is interesting that throughout the book, he calls his friend "Pouder" when in fact, the man's name was listed in the official roster as Andrew Powder.—Ed. 2017

He has raised a family of two sons and one daughter; all are married and are members of the Church of Christ, and all are well respected in the community where they live.

Comrade Pouder tells me that I have exerted quite an influence over him for good in exhorting him to remain steadfast in the faith that was once delivered to the saints, of which, of course, I feel justly proud. And it encourages me to think that perhaps after all I have not lived my life in vain.

In a few days, my burns healed up nicely, and I was able to travel, but I had to wait until others would be able to go, as the officers did not care to bother getting transportation for just one. I was careless about writing home, thinking my people would see by the papers that I was rescued; then, again, I kept thinking I would be forwarded every day, but finally, about the first of May, I sat down and wrote a few lines home, from which I make a few extracts:

"Adams' General Hospital No. 3,

"Memphis, Tennessee, May 1, 1865.

"My Dear Parents:

"Again am I permitted to seat myself to write you a few lines to let you know I am still alive, although I came very near death in that terrible wreck of the *Sultana*, of which I suppose you have read the particulars in the papers. Perhaps you think I was lost, unless you saw in the paper where I was saved.

"I gave my name and regiment to a reporter a short time after I was rescued, so have been a little careless about writing to you all.

"I shall not try to describe to-you all the awful scenes that passed before my eyes that terrible morning, for it would be impossible for me to do so with pen and ink. I will wait till I get home to tell you what I can by word of mouth.

"I made my escape from the burning wreck on one of the large stage planks; drifted to an old stable that was surrounded by water; remained there an hour or two, and was rescued by a boat and brought to Memphis.

"I was slightly burned on face, neck, hands, feet and left arm, but they are all healing very nicely, and I am now able to leave here, but will have to wait till others are able to go with me. It seems hard to get out of a hospital when you once get in one. I will have to wait three or four days yet, and perhaps longer, but will leave here as soon as possible.

"There were at least sixteen hundred lives lost by the explosion. I understand there were 30 of the 50th aboard, and so far I have not heard of but ten that were rescued.

"Oh! to just think of the men that were there rushed into eternity without a moment's warning. I fear that but very few of them were prepared to meet their God. What a warning it should be to us all.

"I close now, hoping to be with you all in a few days.

"With best wishes to all I remain,

"Your affectionate son, Erastus Winters."

Time hung heavy on my hands now in the hospital among strangers, but I passed the most of it in reading good books. One book that I reading while here was the *Life of General John C. Fremont*. It was very interesting to me.

I passed so much of my time reading that I drew the attention of the young lady that was a nurse there at that time, and when there were some ladies from the Christian Commission rooms came in one day with a bundle of religious papers to distribute, the young lady nurse pointed me out to them, telling them I was a great reader. After that I had all the reading matter I wanted.

The Government at Washington made an effort about this time to ferret out who was to blame for the overloading of the *Sultana*, and her final destruction, causing the loss of so many precious lives, but I don't think the investigation ever amounted to anything definite.

A gentleman passed through the hospital one day while I was there, and questioned all the survivors, asking them if they overheard any conversation among the officers of the boat in regard to her being overloaded, or her condition otherwise. When they questioned the man on the cot next to mine he said, "Yes, I heard the Captain say he was going to run the boat through to her destination, or blow her to hell."

I don't know what use the gentleman made of this answer. The poor comrade died from the effects of his burns a few nights afterwards. Poor man; he suffered terribly; he had inhaled the hot steam and was burnt inwardly, as well as scalded outwardly. He was flighty, and talked incessantly the night he died up to within a few moments of his death.

He may have heard the Captain of the *Sultana* make that declaration, and ye tit might not have had any significance, as captains of steamboats are liable to say anything. The captain of the *Sultana* was lost; I never heard of the recovery of his body.

A remarkable escape from the wrecked boat was that of Comrade Daniel McLeod, of St. Louis. He had formerly been a member of the 18th Illinois Volunteer Infantry, and was somewhat lame in his right leg, having received a musket ball in his knee at Pittsburg Landing.

He was a passenger on the *Sultana*, en route from New Orleans to St. Louis. At the time of the explosion he was sitting at a table in the cabin reading a book. He was blown over the table, and had both legs broken at the ankles. He took off his suspenders, and tying them tight above the broken places, dragged himself out, and a Captain of the 54th Ohio helped him down to the lower deck, and then he climbed down the log, chains and let himself into the water, and floated down some two miles, and landed in the brush on Cheek's Island, above Memphis, and in the morning was picked up and brought into the hospital where I was. The surgeon in charge cut off his right limb above the old wound, and when I left the hospital he was getting along fine.

He laughingly told me that the first thing he remembered doing after the explosion was taking his two hands and feeling to see if he still had his head. He said he had been brought up near the water and was a good swimmer. I think his escape in that condition was marvelous.

Growing tired of the hospital one day I got a pass and walked out to see the town. I ran across the Christian Commission rooms and, going in, I penciled the following letter to my sister:

"U. S. Christian Commission Rooms.

"Memphis, Tennessee, May 10, 1865.

"Dear Sister:

"I embrace the present opportunity of writing you a few lines to let you know I am yet alive and well. I am still in Adams' General Hospital at Memphis, but got a pass this morning, and happening to see the Christian Commission rooms, thought I would drop in and jot you down a few lines, and let you know the Lord still sees fit to spare my poor, unprofitable life.

"I wrote father and mother a few days ago, so I suppose you have heard from me by this time. I am getting along fine-; my burns are nearly all healed up, and I think I shall start up the river again in a few days. Well, I don't care how soon, for I am getting uneasy about you all, having heard nothing from any of you since your letter of March 6th, and you know a great deal could happen in that time.

"But I think now, the Lord willing, I shall be home in a short time. We are having delightful weather here now. and I would enjoy a boat ride up the river very much, provided I was not blown up again, which I pray the Lord may never happen me again.

"I want to get home in time for strawberries, if I can. They are plentiful here, but they don't do me any good, as I have no money.

"I will close now, hoping to meet you all in a few days alive and well. I am, dear sister, your affectionate but absent brother.

"Erastus Winters.

"The U. S. Christian Commission sends this as the soldier's messenger to his home. Let it hasten to those who wait for tidings."

After penning these few lines I once more walked out into town, and about twelve o'clock I stepped into the Soldiers' Rest and asked for dinner. They wanted to know where I belonged; I answered them in Adams' Hospital; they said it was against the rules for them to feed men from the hospital, but I explained to them that I had been in there several days, and was tired of the place; that I had a pass, and did not wish to return there till evening and that I had no money, was hungry, and wanted my dinner.

"All right," they answered. "You shall have it. Come right in, and be seated." And they made their word good. They set before me a splendid dinner, and I did it full justice. Thanking them kindly, I started out to visit the park, but on the way there I met a young man from the hospital, who said to me: "Say, if you want to go home you better report to the hospital right away, and get a suit of clothes, as they want to send a squad of you fellows off on the first boat up the river." Said I: "That's me," and you may be sure I was not many minutes getting to the hospital and putting in my order for a suit of Uncle Sam's blue. In a short time, with six or seven other *Sultana* survivors, was fully rigged, furnished transportation and, stepping aboard the fine steamer *Marble City*, were soon steaming northward again on the broad bosom of the Father of Waters.

ARRIVE AT HOME

We had a very pleasant trip from Memphis to Cairo, but we *Sultana* boys would jump every time the engineer would try his water gauges, fearing another explosion.

We arrived at Cairo the evening of May 12th, and put up at the Soldiers' Rest to await transportation by rail to Columbus, Ohio. We called at the rooms of the Christian Commission, and were kindly received. We each penned a short note to friends at home to let them know we were once more on the move towards that longed-for haven of rest.

The people at the Christian Commission rooms told us to call on them when we were ready to leave and they would give us warm meal tickets.

Here follows a copy of the brief note that I penned at that time.

"Christian Commission Rooms,

"Cairo, Ill., May 13, 1865.

"My Dear Parents:

"Once more am I permitted to seat myself to pen you a few brief lines to inform you of my present whereabouts, which you will see at a glance at the top of this sheet. I left Memphis three days ago, and arrived here yesterday evening. Six or seven of us *Sultana* survivors are stopping at the Soldiers' Rest, awaiting transportation by the way of the Illinois Central Railroad to Columbus, Ohio. I think we will leave here tomorrow. We had a very pleasant trip from Memphis here on the steamer *Marble City*. It is a fine boat, and we were not crowded, as there was but few soldiers aboard.

"I am in very good health at present, and hope you are all enjoying the same blessing. If the Lord spares my life, I trust I shall meet you all at home in a few more days.

"I am as ever. Your affectionate son,

"Erastus Winters."

On the way from Memphis to Cairo, having an extra pair of pants, I sold them and going to one of the boat hands I bought an extra supper for my squad. Of course, he had to be a little sly about bringing it to us, and we also had to be a little shady about eating it. But all the same he brought us a good supper, and we ate it and enjoyed it very much. We had plenty of Government rations with us, but we felt like we wanted something more palatable.

We remained at Cairo a day or two, but finally one morning we received our transportation and bidding the Soldiers' Rest goodbye, we started for the depot.

We did not forget to stop at the Christian Commission rooms, and they kept their word by giving each one of us a warm meal ticket, and instructed us that wherever our train stopped for the passengers to get their supper, our tickets would be good for our suppers also. Thanking them for their kindness, we bade them good-bye, and were soon aboard the train steaming toward our destination.

Along in the evening we stopped at some town in Illinois for supper. I took my squad to the door of the dining hall, and inquired of the proprietor if our tickets were good there, and he answered me, "No, sir." I do not know if my men heard his answer or not, but I turned to the squad and said, "Come on, boys," and we all filed in and took seats at the table, and all did ample justice to the fine supper that was placed before us.

Supper finished, we marched out, passed the proprietor, and handed him our tickets, and he never changed a word with us. Of course, the tickets were good for the money, and I knew it, but the proprietor did not want the trouble of collecting the money on them, so he thought he would bluff me. But that was one time his little game of bluff did not come his way.

Reseating ourselves in the cars, we were soon on the move again. I got very weary and sleepy after midnight, and snatched a few winks of sleep as we steamed along.

As daylight appeared, we were nearing Indianapolis, and received the cheering news that Jeff Davis had been captured, arrayed in petticoats. This news raised quite an excitement on the train, and we began to think now that surely peace was near for our unhappy country.

In due time we arrived at Columbus, Ohio, and my squad was sent out to Camp Chase. I have always been sorry that I did not keep a list of the names of those boys that came through with me from Memphis to Columbus, but we were all thinking more about getting home at that time than anything else, so we lost sight of each other at Camp Chase, to meet no more in this world, for I think it is quite likely they have all answered the last roll call. But I hope to meet them again when we fall in for that grand Inspection on the other shore.

On my arrival at Camp Chase I had the good fortune to meet Comrades Jack Culp and Alex McCradie, of Co. "K." They had been mustered and received some pay, but the mustering officer was gone when I arrived there, so I received no money while there.

Coming up the Mississippi, I had eaten a little too hearty of cocoanuts; my stomach being weak, the nuts were too rich for me, and now at Camp Chase the drinking cups at all the wells were cocoanut shells. I could hardly drink the water out of them, and have never had much use for cocoanuts since.

Knowing now that I was to be discharged and sent home, the time passed very slowly; every day seemed a week long.

McCradie and I took a notion to have some eggs one day, so we purchased about two dozen, and also half a pound of butter. The butter was strong enough to walk, if it could have been furnished with legs and feet, and it was not the bald-headed quality either. We borrowed a kettle from one of the cooks, and soon had our eggs cooking.

We got some bread, salt and pepper, and prepared to have our feast. Well, we boiled the eggs till they were blue as indigo and hard enough to use for base balls; then we sat down and feasted. And I wonder today yet how we ever lived to get home after eating that mess. If those eggs had been in my stomach when I was trying to swim the Mississippi, I am sure these reminiscences would never have been written, for the author would have gone to the bottom like a chunk of lead.

I am glad to have it to say that Comrade McCradie arrived home safe, got married, and raised a large family, but am sorry to say that when I visited him at his home in Millville, Ohio, in 1904, the poor man was dying by inches; a cancer on the side of his head was eating his life away. This is August, 1905; I have not heard from the comrade for about five months, but from his condition then I think it likely he has answered the last roll call and passed over the dark river.

On Saturday, the 20th of May, I received an honorable discharge from the United States Service by an order from the War Department dated, I think. May 11th, and Comrade Culp and I came to Columbus and boarded a train for Cincinnati, which place we reached Sunday morning, May 21st, just as the dawn began to light up the eastern sky.

Comrade Culp's home was at Ironton, Lawrence County, Ohio, but as it was Sunday there was no boat up the river before Monday, so after getting our breakfast I invited Comrade Culp to go home with me to Ludlow, Kentucky, and remain till Monday. He gladly accepted the invitation, and it was not many minutes until I was at home, sweet home.

I learned by inquiry soon after crossing the river at the Ludlow or Fifth Street Ferry that my people at home were all well, and that filled my heart with joy and thankfulness.

I shall not try to describe my feelings as I drew near the old home. At last I am in sight of the door, and saw my two little nephews standing out in the front.

As soon as they caught sight of two boys in blue approaching they skipped into the house and told my mother. In a moment she appeared in the doorway and began clapping her hands for joy and gladness, and as I quickly reached her she clasped me in those blessed arms and pressed me to her motherly breast.

Dear, kind God! Blessed mother! Who can tell what a heavy burden of care, anxiety and trouble rolled off that motherly heart at that moment, and what a wave of joy and gladness took its place?

I went into the army against my mother's will, and had she died before my return I would always have regretted it. But thank God! He spared both of our lives to meet in a grand reunion. Father and sister were at church when I arrived, and they came in directly, and then what a happy reunion we had. What a warm greeting I received from one and all.

I was in my old home once more, and was surrounded by loved ones. What a happy boy I was! The suffering and privations of the last five months were for the time forgotten. I was a free boy or man again; free to go and come where and when I pleased, and no one could say me nay. There were no guards to bother me, and there was no dead line around me. I was free as the air as long as I kept within the bounds of the law.

Home again! What a sweet thought that was to me. Home again, surrounded by loved ones and friends, who were vying with each other to do me honor. All were anxious to hear me tell of the marches I had made, the battles I had been in, my prison experience and, last though not least, they wanted to hear my story of the *Sultana* wreck, and how I made my escape.

Monday morning I went with Comrade Culp to the steamboat landing to see him off, and then bade him good-bye. I have never met him since, but heard he arrived home safe. Comrade Culp had a kind heart when he let whisky alone, but, like many others when under its influence, it would cause him to mistreat his best friends.

Monday evening a bevy of six young ladies called to see me, prompted by curiosity, of course. Now the reader may think that the experience I had passed through, and the trials and hardships that had come my way in the past three years ought to have knocked all the timidity and bashfulness out of me, but I am sorry to have to put it on record that it had not; and when they told me I must go in and face that delegation of ladies I felt as though I would sooner face one of General Hood's masked batteries of twenty-pound rifled Parrot guns.

In fact, I felt like calling for a pick and shovel and digging a gopher hole for myself and crawling into it. Where now was all my boasted nerve and courage? Gone glimmering. But like the soldier under fire for the first time, I pulled myself together and entered the room, and as I stepped across the threshold six pairs of eyes were focused on me and I felt myself blushing to the very roots of my red hair.

And to make it still more trying on my nerves, they were all strangers to me. I had to be presented to each one of them personally. Talk about charging forts, batteries and breastworks! Why, the ordeal that I had to pass through in that room in the few moments that it consumed to present me to the owners of those six pairs of eyes required more real courage than it did to charge the rebel rifle pits in front of Atlanta, Georgia.

I never could tell how I got through it all; it made me feel all over in spots as big as a United States army blanket. I managed to get through some way, and found myself still living.

One of the ladies, a fine, portly lass, seemed to take delight in causing me to feel still more embarrassed by her cruel shafts of wit, directed at me, of course, in a spirit of mischief. But I lived to see the day when I more than got even with her, and we became very intimate friends.

But notwithstanding the raid those bright eyes made on me I was happy; I was at home in God's country, under the bright folds of Old Glory and, best of all, the white dove of peace was again hovering over our beautiful country.

The hostile armies that had been fighting each other for four years were now being disbanded and sent to their homes, to take up again their respective vocations that they laid aside when they entered the service.

Our sympathies go out to those who wore the grey, who bravely marched and fought under the Stars and Bars for a cause their leaders made them believe was just and right.

Let us not be harsh with them; they have been deceived; the right has triumphed, and those who fought so bravely under the Stars and Bars have been compelled to lay down their arms and see their flag lowered in the dust and to hear their leaders say, "Our cause is lost."

They see Old Glory, the grand old Stars and Stripes, the banner of the free, floating freely over every State in the Union once more.

The common soldiers under the Stars and Bars that were in the ranks and did the fighting are not so much to blame. Poor men! Many of them were thrown upon the world, without a home and without a penny. Let us be lenient towards them; let us welcome them back into the Union like our nobler Lincoln, with charity for all and malice toward none.

Even our glorious old flag, the Red, White and Blue, as she displays her beautiful colors in the bright May sunlight seems to say "Let us have peace" but the leaders who brought all this misery and suffering not only , on their beautiful Southland but also on the Northland, will receive their reward—if not in this world, surely in that which is to come.

Those never-to-be-forgotten May days passed by on eagle's wings as I swung around the circle, visiting my relatives and friends. Everywhere I was greeted with a warm welcome, and everyone tried to rival the others in doing me honor, and I was no exception as my old comrades who may read this can verify.

We who wore the blue were received at home with glad hearts and were given a royal welcome by every lover of our dear old flag, and none of us will ever forget while we live those happy days. Forty years have passed by since the eventful spring of 1865.

What giant strides our glorious country has made! When Spain had the boldness to insult our flag, what did we see? We saw the young men of the Southland rally as quickly to wipe out the insult as did their Northern brothers; and more, we saw some of the very leaders who wore the gray and fought bravely for the lost cause from '61 to '65 step quickly to the front and volunteer to lead their sons to victory under the protecting folds of Old Glory.

They were proud and anxious to wear the blue, and did wear it with honor, and while we still have a few in the North as well as the South who hold malice, and have a bitter feeling against each other, yet, thank God, it is fast dying out.

And whether we look to the East, West, North or South, we see a united and prosperous country, all under one flag, and that flag honored and respected on every land and sea, and we of that grand old Grand Army of the Republic are proud that we were the humble instruments in the hands of a just God to make this possible.

(Yes, this country owes the honor of what it now enjoys to us whose ranks are thinning, the old Grand Army boys.)

Our numbers are fast decreasing, day by day, as the years pass by. Soon, ah! how soon will the last member of the Grand Army of the Republic be gone, and that grandest organization this world ever saw will have passed into history, but as we go hence we will have the comforting assurance that we have tried to instill into the minds of our children a true spirit of patriotism, and feel that in the hands of our sons the honor of the country and flag will be safe.

The Grand Army of the Republic was the Union veterans organization. It was dissolved in 1956 when its last member, Albert Woolson (1850–1956) of Duluth, Minnesota, died.—Ed. 2017

In the forty years that have come and gone since the great Civil War came to a close the writer has witnessed many changes. He has lived in an age when many improvements have been made. Inventions after inventions have come to the front, until we are almost forced to conclude that there is nothing so hidden but what the ingenuity of man will search it out and compel it to do his bidding.

Yes, we are living in an age of inventions and improvements. A fast age, for millions are won and lost in a day. Our nation is enjoying an era of prosperity that has never been surpassed by any other nation under Heaven.

And I sometimes wonder if this great success, this great prosperity that we, as a nation, are now enjoying, will not prove our ruin. Will we in our pride, haughtiness and selfishness, forget the All-wise God who rules over the destinies of nations? Will we not in our mad race for prominence and riches neglect to render to him that homage which is His due, and will it not cause Him to bring a curse upon us?

God help us to be more humble in his sight, and not to think of ourselves more highly than we ought to think.

As for my own life personally since the close of our great civil strife, I have had a checkered career. I have seen both the dark and bright side of life. I have known what it was to be happy and what it was to be cast down with sorrows and sadness.

While I was blessed with the good fortune of being happily married three times, yet I was unfortunate in that I lost each wife by death after enjoying a period of happiness with each. I have raised four daughters and one son, of whom any father might well feel proud. They are a comfort to me as I travel down toward the sunset of life.

Unhappily though, by my misfortunes, I have not been permitted to extend to them that care and help that it would have been my delight had I been blessed with the means.

Having no education and no trade, I had to carve my way through life, principally by common labor, and meeting the reverses I have, I did not succeed in accumulating any of this world's goods.

I have tried in my weak way to do my duty to God and to my fellow man, as I saw it, believing that a good name was more to be desired than riches.

As I look back over my life, I can see I have made many mistakes that had I my life to live over again, with the experience I now have, I certainly would try to avoid, but this can never be.

The past is gone beyond recall. I can only hope that I may be forgiven for the mistakes of the past, and pray God that He may so direct my future steps that I may always be found walking in that narrow way that leads to eternal happiness.

And now I must bring my little story to a close, and it is almost with regret that I write it.

While some of the scenes I have tried in my blundering way to describe were very sad, others were pleasant; all of them in the hands of one who was well educated and a fluent writer could have been made very interesting, but I have done the best I could under the circumstances to entertain my readers, and I trust, in the kindness of their hearts, they will pardon my shortcomings and overlook my rude way of expressing myself, and this I believe they will readily do when they consider the source.

I pen these concluding lines on my sixty-second birthday. I well know that long ago in the journey of life I passed over the heights and am now traveling down the western slope towards the sunset. A lonely old veteran, I wait and listen for the final call of the Orderly who shall summon me to answer the last roll call.

May the Father above help me to so live the remainder of my days that I shall pass the final inspection and be considered worthy to stand in the ranks of that grand army above on the shore of the beautiful river, where God himself shall be the Supreme Commander, is my prayer.

Kind reader, my task is finished. If I have succeeded in helping you to pass a pleasant hour or two while reading these reminiscences, I shall feel myself amply repaid for my labor.

CORPORAL ERASTUS WINTERS.

THE END

DISCOVER MORE LOST HISTORY AT BIGBYTEBOOKS.COM

Made in the USA
Monee, IL
30 January 2021